DEEP ROOTS
OF THE
SOUL

DEEP ROOTS OF THE SOUL

Soaring for Healing

TAMMY HENSON

Deep Roots of the Soul
Copyright © 2015 by Tammy Henson. All rights reserved.
No part of this publication may be reproduced, stored in a retrieval system or transmitted in any way by any means, electronic, mechanical, photocopy, recording or otherwise without the prior permission of the author except as provided by USA copyright law.

The opinions expressed by the author are not necessarily those of Revival Waves of Glory Books & Publishing.

Revival Waves of Glory Books & Publishing
PO Box 596
Litchfield, IL 62056
United States of America
www.revivalwavesofgloryministries.com

Revival Waves of Glory Books & Publishing is committed to excellence in the publishing industry.

Published in the United States of America

Ebook: 978-1-312-76201-5
Paperback: 978-1542514323
Hardcover: 978-1-312-76199-5

Table of Contents

LITTLE GIRL LOST	6
A SOUL THAT CRIES	7
ENCOUNTER OF HIS LOVE	9
GOD'S PRAYER MOVEMENT	11
THE NATIONS	13
LAID UP WEALTH	15
RIVERS OF LIVING WATER	17
STORMY DAYS	20
WHAT DO I SAY…	22
MY FRIEND	24
POTTER VS. CLAY	26
MY SOUL LONGS	27
IN THESE LAST DAYS	28
GOD'S CORRECTION	30
WARING FOR PROMISES	31
SOUL TIES	33
GENERATIONAL CURSE	34
YOUR PLAN – NOT MINE	36
DENIAL OF HIS POWER	38
NEW YEAR	40
FORGIVING SELF	42
"SEEKING"	44
THE ROAD	46
ANGER	48
BROKEN MOLD	51
BROKEN ROAD	53
FINGERPRINTS	54
FACE TO FACE	56
THIS PLACE…	58
THE CLEAR MESSAGE	60
Other Books By Tammy Henson	62

LITTLE GIRL LOST

I'm a little girl lost
    A damaged soul was the cost

Many buyers to throw the dart
    I've been ripped apart

I've stuffed rejection and loneliness – down so deep
    The coals are a burning heap

The stabbing pair leaves me down
    I look up and say god; all I want is a crown

I'm weak and sore
    The root rotten to the core

Breaking the chair of long-suffering is in god's hand
    The tears rest in the deserts land

Where do I go from here?
    I need you Lord to interfere

I don't know the answer but you do
    Where's freedom in what I go through

I lay it at your feet
    Hoping your touch will greet

A little girl lost
    Dried up in the frost

It's dark and it's cold
    Come heal this broken heart I hold

A SOUL THAT CRIES

A soul that cries
    A soul that searches w/no surprise

A soul that reaches behind
    But finds no rest in the mind

From birth the soul screams out
    With a loud shout

Love me; take care of me; & hold me
    The soul recognizes the need to be

Comforted, accepted & loved
    But it takes years to know it only comes From God above

He made us to need these things
    But at denying Christ we deny the things only he can bring

We look for it in people, things & places
    But the result is pain, and tears in the faces

The soul becomes wounded & scared
    Pierced & marred

It's not until we invite Jesus into our lives
    That we heal and that love thrives

So if you're searching cry out
    Because there's no doubt

It is written in a Psalm
    He heals the broken heart & binds up their wounds So let
    God sing you a new song

A song of healing in your heart
    A song where peace is the start

An intimate relationship is what it's about
    So look to him and cry out

Embrace Jesus' touch
    Because he loves you so much

He knows about every tear and every hurt
    He knows about every evil work

He knows what's been done to you
    He wants to heal, that's what he wants to do

He's waiting, on you to say the word
    Jesus come into my heart

Love me, heal me and embrace me
    Shine your face and let me see

And everything will reverse
    Blessing instead of curse

ENCOUNTER OF HIS LOVE

Fragrance and incense sent
    The beauty of sacrifice went

I brought with me a rose
    And laid it on his toes

The oil of heaven came to me
    As sweet myrrh estered me to be

In a beautiful relationship with my King
    You're his bride I heard the angels sing

Come into the place
    Prepared for you to see his face

Sit at the table for the lords embrace
    Come into this heavenly place

The color of love is red
    The sight of love is fresh bread

The sound of love is his soft voice
    The touch of love is our rejoice

As his presence flooded the room
    I saw a vision of the tomb

I saw chains being broken
    By Jesus; one word spoken

The power of his love
    I saw as my spirit rose above

To an intimate place of fate
    Of love at Heaven's gate

GOD'S PRAYER MOVEMENT

Prayer in the midst of men
    has hit an all time low what a sin

It's written pray without ceasing
    it's commanded; so why is it decreasing

Rejoice, give thanks and pray
    Gods looking for pray movements today

We want him to answer our cry
    but were not moving that's why

His power has decreased
    let's wake up and release

The glory presence in this hour
    let's reach out for his power

God's looking for a people to dedicate
    because the church has lost it's fate

Arise and shine; his glory is upon you
    deep intimacy is where it shines through

Less of me, more of Him
    that's where the holy ghost wants to begin

Put off self
    put your plans on the shelf

He wants us day and night
    to worship him; that's right

Seven days a week
    To be humble and meek

Our own agenda and plan
    Brings about he works of man

He's looking for a Jesus people
    To open up the steeple

Monday – Sunday
    Listen to what the words have to say

We need to intercede
    Because it's his commandment and our deed

So let's come together and pray
    Each and every day

THE NATIONS

Were in trouble, the nation
    were breaking our vows of relation

There's a sound of vibration
    against God in the infiltration

America is out of order
    we through God back to the border

Lack of knowledge and no vision
    we've shut our ears, we will not listen

God has sent the warning
    speaking and for warning

"O" how this nation
    has turned the rotation

It's written there will be signs
    of the end times

Blood, fire and billows of smoke
    it's our fault, the nation is broke

We did it; we denied the foundation
    of what started this nation

He's trying to give us a second chance
    to give him a glance

Blessing or curse
    what will be our immerse

We get to choose our fate
   repent before it's too late

Homosexuality, abortion and hate
   we are captured as satan's bait

It's an abomination
   why are we accepting this sin

You hear about it; on the news
   being accepted as new moves

We as Christians need to take a stand
   against politicians in our land

Because God is about to withdrawal his hand
   and when he does

He will close his ear
   and our cries he will not hear

This is a warning for the nation
   it's time to cry out for God's salvation.

LAID UP WEALTH

The wealth of the sinner is laid up for the just
    God's moving lack into the sinners dust

God's about to show up
    Filling up our cup

There's a move of God coming in this hour
    With full fledge power

People will know who we are
    He's about to raise the bar

Money will come into our hands
    As it's released from heaven's strands

We as God's people will stand out
    God's going to bless, as angels shout

The sinner will be broke
    As we are released from the yoke

People will know us, by our God
    Because of his mighty rod

Were entering into a season
    Where the waters will deepen

The rivers will flow
    And the trumpets will blow

A season of plenty for the just
    As the winds gust

All of the sudden increase
    As the sinners decrease

God's not going to be silent
    He's about to get violent

It is written; the violent take it by force
    God's about to reset the course

Heaven is about to open the window
    His glory is about to show

People of God get ready
    God's releasing heavens machete

Were in a war
    But God's about to shut the door

Were about to win
    This war of sin

RIVERS OF LIVING WATER

Come to the water
    My beloved daughter

Come to the river
    Come do the Holy Ghost shiver

Come into the secret place
    Come in and taste

The glory river fountain
    Come up to the mountain

Where the presence is the Lord
    Coming on you as one accord

Come and eat with me
    Come let the light shine free

Take communion; eat of the bread
    For His body that was bruised and Blood shed

Drink of this wine
    For I am His and He is mine

Come to the living water and thirst no more
    Soak as you lay on the floor

Wait for him to fall on you
    As revelation carries you to

A new realm of the spirit
    I hear the sound of the river, don't quit

Quiet the flesh the anointing is here
    Silence the mind go into the atmosphere

Go into Shekinah Glory's abode
    Let a habitation unfold

Go into the secret place
    Sit at his feet and touch his face

Go down into the deep and get the key
    Let spiritual eye's see

Heaven's waiting to be revealed
    Go into this beautiful field

Where angels dance
    And the elders worship in a trance

Go join the choir of heavens voice
    Lift your hands and rejoice

Be still as Jesus releases
    And the spirit teaches

Open your eyes come back still
    Let his presence fill

The place you reside
    Let not the power divide

Walk with the fire and power
    In this crucial hour

Let the supernatural flow
    Let the power show

Manifestations shall come to earth
    As a new move is birthed

Heaven will shine down
 As the miracles hit your town

There will be no denying the signs
 When the glory shines

STORMY DAYS

Be calm in the storm
    Be gentle and warm

You will see better days
    Look through the Smokey haze

Hang on and don't give up
    There's breakthrough coming, he's going to fill your cup

The stormy weather is about to clean
    Get up and look in the mirror

Yes it's been a hard road
    Yes you have carried a heavy load

The walk has been dreary
    The mind has been Leary

Things have been hindered and broke
    Child I'm removing the yoke

The way is being made
    For your foundation to be laid

There are many open doors
    That was closed before

The season is ripe, and it is time
    Because the fruit is on the vine

I'm calling you into something great
    It's destiny; it's fate

Say goodbye to the hardship
  The page is about to flip

The affliction of your soul
  It's time to shake, rattle & roll

Mighty & powerful, you will be
  Remove the veil and see, this beautiful picture I have you thee

WHAT DO I SAY...

As I walk by the people on the street
    I realize; you never know whom you will meet

I see pain in there eye's
    And my soul cries

I think to myself, what can I say
    To make the pain go away

I quickly realize that used to be me
    This deep pain I see

I hit the bottomless pit
    Where Jesus' light was lit

I know pain and I know love
    I know the results of the mask & glove

Hiding behind the things of this age
    The drugs, and the rage

The hurt and the pain
    A life lived in vain

But today I stand speechless on the street
    As I see souls in defeat

I want to reach out
    Inside I scream & shout

What do I say
    To a hurting world, in such disarray

I know where the answer lies
   For a soul that dies

How can I get a changed mind?
   How can I get them find?

How can I get them to see:
   That only Jesus can make them free

My tongue is tied
   For a world that needs to abide

"O" Jesus opens up a well in me today
   So you can have your way

MY FRIEND

In my life, I had one true friend
    Like a sister, she stuck by me, till the end

Friends since we were young
    Then one day God said; your done

It was the hardest thing I ever did
    But the Lord forbid

I cried day and night
    She was my heart and my delight

I didn't understand, neither did she
    But God was putting a foundation in me

I see her from time to time
    My how her face would shine

I would sit and cry over her beauty
    But I had a Christian duty

To surrender to my Lord
    This friendship; he cut the cord

It's been over a year
    O the countless tears

I think about her, my heart is broke
    But today he said the sentence is revoked

He said I'm doing a new thing
    A friendship saved by the king

I take away
  But I also can brighten the day

I do things according to my will
  A friendship like this, I will heal

I separated for a reason
  But I call it back in this season

The purpose is so grand
  Love is the demand

The beauty of the way it used to be
  It will shine, just wait and see

POTTER VS. CLAY

He is the potter I am the clay
    Such a sacrifice I must pay

Half the work belongs to me
    An obedient child I must be

He does what I cannot do
    It's him that brings me through

Through the fire, I must go
    "O" those trials to make me white as snow

The tribulations to purify
    So him I can glorify

It is such a pain
    The hardships, so he can train

He is the potter; I am the clay
    I look towards heaven as I pray

Lord life the pressure from my back
    Help me Lord, through this lack

He says child it's a test
    To bring you to your very best

Soon the rewards will come to pass
    And when they do it will happen fast

So hold on a little longer
    This will make you stronger

MY SOUL LONGS

My soul longs for this generation to see;
    The Lord in fear, my heart hurts within me

To see a people so lost
    When victory stands out the cross

The foolishness of a generation so blind
    I pray Lord, somehow you they would find

You love the prodigal son; for he doesn't know
    The reassurance of that love that was sown

Lord I ask for revelation to cover
    Let your spirit hover

Over a nation so full of itself
    Bring restoration and bring health

Bring our beating hearts
    To a place where sin departs

Make us a generation so humble
    Make us strong; not to stumble

My soul longs for this generation to be turned back to you
    Lord please have mercy in everything you do

Give us grace
    Cause this generation to seek your face

IN THESE LAST DAYS

I watched the news today
    Quit alarming I must say

The devil really has a hold
    But in the word it was foretold

That in the last days
    There will be scoffers, who lust in their own ways

Look around your city
    Your heart should be full of pity

Same sex marriage has been
    Accepted by all men

What happened to our pledge
    No wonder were on edge

About to cave
    America we need saved

Abortion is at an all-time height
    These innocent baby's don't deserve to die

They have been seen running away
    From the vacuums ray

They can feel the pain of their legs and arms being decapitated
    America this should be hated

Where have we went wrong
    Rebellious is our new song

Lovers of self; it is written
     The love of God has been smitten

People get ready for this war
     Disobedience has opened the door

For the enemy to come in
     To destroy the works of man

God did say
     Not to live this way

But we chose to rebel
     We are in danger of the flames of hell

It's written in the book
     Open it and look

GOD'S CORRECTION

I discipline and correct
    So I can perfect

Though it may bring pain
    It's done in love not in vain

It's grievous and holds no joy
    Countless tears I must employ

I must lose it all
    For destiny to call

Everything I hold dear
    For God to draw near

I must deny
    My flesh must die

To gain his will not mine
    Our spirits must combine

To give it away
    It's my price to pay

To be humble and to agree
    So my soul can be free

It's a loss for a gain
    My life I put at the cross

I lay it down
    To have heavens crown

WARING FOR PROMISES

The enemy said it's not gonna get better
    Put away prophecy's letter

He fights and wages the attack
    To keep you in the trap of lack

God has a great plan
    "O" but the enemy will take a stand

He will try to get you to miss the mark
    So in this war we must embark

It requires much for God's blessings to touch we must wave
    For the promises, we must improve

Passing the tests
    Before it can rest

We must stand in the fire
    To get that which we desire

It won't just come, it has a price
    Yes it sounds lovely and nice

But we have to break & defeat
    The enemy as we put him under our feet

The prophecy's you've heard are true
    There special blessings just for you

Look at the enemy, tell him to move out of your way
    Look at him and say

Devil; you're a liar and I'm laying hold
    Tell him double portion; tell him two fold

Get up on your feet and war
    So you can walk through the open door

SOUL TIES

The attack rages
    As the war wages

Revelation Lord I ask
    He rebuked the demonic mask

He removed the blindness so I could see
    The soul ties standing in front of me

My soul was lost in other's souls
    "O" how this took a toll

I must shut this dark door
    The curse; pain it bore

I must take my soul back
    To cancel the spirit of lack

I break every witchcraft
    I plead the blood against the shaft

I bind and loose this tie I cut your head, you must die I suffocate
    the enemies attack
    My soul I take it back

GENERATIONAL CURSE

My family tree
    your generations coming at me

What is a generational curse
    Identifying this must come first

Spiritual bondage; sins of my fore fathers what must I do
    To get that demon to pass through

A generation stronghold
    How do I break the mold

It must stop here
    The depression and the fear

I must repent
    For the sins the enemy sent

I must break the chain
    Of the sins that were lain

The cycle I bare
    From the enemies snare

My family tree
    For my children and me

I ask forgiveness for every sin
    I cancel every curse, from beginning to end

I plead the blood over every curse
    Let your fire immerse

Now I confess
    Instead of curse I'm blessed

Thank you Jesus from the bottom of my heart
    For every curse that does depart

YOUR PLAN – NOT MINE

Lord I repent and I confess
    For not doing my very best

I jumped off the road into my own plan
    I let go of your hand

I realize your way is the only way
    So Lord I repent, forgive me this day

I just ask you to teach
    As my soul is reached

Teach me to pray
    As in your stillness I lay

Search my heart
    Let all evil depart

Take hold of my mind
    As your spirit searches to find

Bring out the best in me
    "O" Lord set me free

It's not about me; it's about you
    May you will be all I do

Teach me to sing
    To ride on angels wings

Teach me to glide
    To go into your presence to hide

Lord I give you all the glory
    Let my life tell a story

Use me where you can
    Use me a simple man

May I die daily at your feet
    Let your voice be discreet

I surrender I give my life to you
    Whatever you will let me do

Where you go, I will go
    It's the holy spirits flow

Lord I will walk down the street
    Where your who I meet

I give up my plans and take yours as mine
    "O" Lord let us dine

Give me bread – give me wine
    "O" Lord your will I want to find

My life is not my own
    I'm yours, all flesh and bone

Expose every raw area in my soul
    Let your spirit fill the whole

Teach me Lord, don't let me go
    Just train me, allow me to grow

DENIAL OF HIS POWER

There are these spiritual gifts
    But the church, is causing them to sift

The enemy has caused lies to be believed as truth
    He's starting with the youth

It's written do not despise
    Prophecy and rise

The church has a form of Godliness, but denies it's power
    No wonder it's went sour

It's written and we insist it's a lie
    Pay attention to the spirits cry

We are judging with our minds
    Hypocrites is what they find

A generation who hates the house of the Lord
    The enemy has cut love's cord

We criticize and mock
    There's no love for the flock

Witchcraft, jezebel and divination has been living in the church
    Like a bird, sitting on a perch

The lost are being turned away "O" but there's a price to pay
    The mouth of God, is opening in this day

He's had enough he's about to come down
    And take back his ground

My true prophets are being laughed at scorned and burned
    But I the Lord am about to turn

A religious people, to a place
    I'm gonna withdraw my grace

And everyone will know
    The church has become my foe

I'm about to close the door
    Because I want more

Prophecy, healings and the manifested presence of God
    He's going to be adored and awed

Churches will be shut down
    So his glory can be found

I the Lord have spoken
    We must reach the broken

Take this warning & take heed
    Repent and follow my lead

NEW YEAR

This is a new year
    People pay attention and hear

The sound of the river coming down
    The sound of fire hitting your town

Put on the garment of praise
    Because Jesus fire is ablaze

Heaven is about to his earth
    We've hit a growth spurt

Listen to the sound
    Of the motion in the ground

Can you hear it?
    The declarations of the spirit

"O" Holy on of Israel
    Come down, and heal

Bring the honey, bring the Glory for it's a new year
    The sound I hear so clear

I see a basket of fruit
    I hear the rams horn; going toot

The sound of a new wave
    Come Lord mightily for it's you we crave

This new wine
    As a new sign

We need you more than ever before
  I can hear the spirits roar

People get ready it's here
  Worship as it draws near

FORGIVING SELF

The art of forgiving self
    Can cancel sickness and bring health

Emotionally, physically and in the mind
    Forgiveness releases the blind

It causes things to take place
    For healing has a taste

It's tastes sweet not bitter
    Quit letting poison be a transmitter

Forgive and a release your will find
    Leave it all behind

In forgiving yourself, you learn
    To let God's love burn

For yourself and for others
    For your sisters and brothers

Lay it at the cross
    Put it at his feet

Where it will bring (incline)
    Joy in everything

It is written, a merry heart does good like medicine
    But a broken spirit dries the bones

I forgive myself this day
    Give me medicine Lord is you may

Heal my heart of anger & hate
    Come fast, don't make me wait

I'm ready for your touch
    Embrace me Lord; love me much

Flood it in like the waters flood the ground
    I am no longer bound

I forgive myself today
    "O" thank you Jesus for teaching me your way

"SEEKING"

In the stillness, I find you
 In the quiet, is where you come through

It's in your presence I find rest
 It's there, in the morning crest

Your voice becomes so clear
 Through the days winds, I hear

I seek you for the days guide
 In your presence our souls are tied

I feel your touch, I feel your embrace
 "O" Lord I seek your face

You are so good
 Come Holy Spirit, if you would

Don't take your spirit from me!
 Come Lord, let me see

Through your eye's
 Where Christ's mind lies

Sculpt and mold
 Comfort and hold

Teach and train
 Dance with me in the rain

This intimacy
 As you draw near

Let your glory appear shine through the cloud
    Blow the trumpets loud

Show up in a might way
    As I seek your face today

THE ROAD

I'm walking down a road
    Carrying many baggage's my what a load

It is all so heavy
    I pray Lord, cause me to be steady

He says the answer is in you child
    Your imagination is going wild

He says keep it simple
    And you won't grow weary and cripple

This journey is not hard
    Nor is it a fun card

There's a balance in all you do
    "O" child let me get you through

Many obstacles along the way
    Don't let it lead you astray

Keep looking forward to your goal
    Stay humble and low

Seek the God of peace
    He'll anoint you with oil; slick as grease

You can do all things
    You're under the shadow of his wings

So this road may swerve a bit
    But it's to keep you strong and fit

Have faith and trust
> Keep your eyes on me it's a must

Pray & seek
> And keep your heart meek

This road might be long
> But you can do it, you are strong

The broken pieces are forming, right
> "O" child you're my glorious light

This road isn't just for you, it's for others to
> To heal and to save, that's what he anointed you to do

So be confident in this
> My glory will shine and bring sweet bliss

Stay on the road
> But let go of that big load

ANGER

There's a hidden place in the depths of my soul
    Where junk burns black as coal

It's hard to realize it's there
    It's rarely seen, it's like the air

Every once in a while I feel the breeze
    That makes my heart freeze

But I don't see or sense
    Or realize angers pinch

Sometimes it's so deep
    The pain has went to sleep

The suppression in your mind
    That's why it's hard to find

There's only one; who can cause
    It to surface

The healer, there's nothing amiss, He digs down real deep
    Because he desires wholeness for his sheep

So next time the wind blows
    Open your heart, don't keep it closed

Wounds get deeper as you keep them hidden open up yourself;
    let him heal
    When he does, seal the deal

The enemy loses yet once again
    As you come against sin

He's loosing little by little every step you take
    Those stepping stones of faith, they make

Is miracles and signs
    As Jesus heals your heart and mind

Come into his saving grace
    "O" come touch his face

Feel it, sense it, and heal
    Notice the warm breeze you feel

The air isn't cold, it's hot
    Your hearts free, never again in a knot

The joy and brightness of your skin
    The happy tears dripping off your chin

The peace
    Feel anger grease

Love is creeping inside
    Let Jesus light shine

Be healed
    As the pain is revealed

Chains be broken
    As the words are spoken

Every hindrance and utterance be shattered
    May the enemy be battered

I curse the yoke
    I command it to be broke

Hoy Spirit come like wild fire
    I come against the liar

I stand up strong
    For it's you only, that I long

BROKEN MOLD

When God breaks you, it shatters into pieces on the floor
    He is making your spirit poor

Reforming you isn't easy or fun
    Its pain until it's done

It's grievous to the bones
    To the soul it moans

But in the end
    You thank God; for the trend

For the new mind
    For the things left behind

When the mold starts to form
    It's the end to the storm

The heart of God, is your gift
    As the old starts to lift

There's a piece of you that has torn
    As the new you birthed and was born

There's a song – sang over you
    For the storm he drug you through

It was hard, and at times hurt; like a knifes blades
    But now sins gone and Christ invades

A work may now begin of the war against sir destiny comes as a
    shining pearl
    Beautiful as a little girl

He's got a plan
    For this race you've ran

Be strong and stand up firm
    Be bold and stern

Thank God for his mold
    And his ailing hold

Fight the good fight
    As you shine your light

On the souls
    It's planted see, where it grows

Good works are to be
    The sight your eyes see

To be the echo you hear
    As Christ is your only pier

BROKEN ROAD

God bless my broken road
    That led me to your hold

Of my sins, of my past
    It's the pain that was cast

That led me into your arms
    Like the sound of an alarm

My past made me who I am this day
    Thank you Jesus for hearts decay

You heal the broken
    It's you; every word spoken

You the reason I live to tell about a life in chains
    Of torment and pains

It led me straight to you thank you Jesus for all you do
    For loving me enough to see me through

For allowing my broken heart
    To lead me to a new start

"O" Lord you heal the broken
    I carry you, like a token

I turned from death
    And you gave me new breath

Thank you
    For the pain you put me through

FINGERPRINTS

(Colors below are Described as the Holy Spirit Speaks
to Author. Colors Mean Something Else to You.)

Every life has fingerprints
    It has proof, and hints

Take a look at their pain
    Look at the fingerprints in the rain

In the storm, or their acts
    There's a knife in there backs

Fingerprints have colors' red
    Is the print of anger?

He needed love not danger green is the print of pride
    He needed noticed, not broken lies

Blue is the print of depression
    He needed gentleness not aggression

Yellow is the print of fear He got pushed away violence
    Is all he could hear?

Gold is the print of greed
    He needed someone to care but instead no one took heed.

Silver is the print of betray
    He suffered night and day

Brown is the print of deadness of spirit
    in His actions you can hear it.

Purple is the print of excessive need
    because it was never met, it's still a dead seed

Black is the print of everything dark
    rejection was the mark

So next time you get hurt by someone, look at the print
    because their life is the hint

Love them care for the soul
    lift them up because their feeling low

It's just there pain crying out,
    it's there soul giving a shout

Be a shield for the broken
    encouragement, let it be spoken

Shine your light
    be someone's delight

FACE TO FACE

The spirit dropped in the room
    The light as bright as the moon

My body soaked in the fragrance of him
    The presence touched every limits

The manifestation of his face
    I was the holy spirits base

As the increase grew
    So did the glory dew

Visitations of a warm liquid form
    As deep intimacy is born

The silence that arose
    In a vision I saw his nose

Then his face; my eyes closed
    Face to face in the unseen realm

Imitating senses of his breath
    This visitation love as strong as death

As I lie there on the floor
    I feel his love embracing me more

So strong; it's threshing my spirit
    The angels are singing I can hear it

Approaching the throne
    As I shake and moan

I loose control of my function
    As the spirit is in unction

I'm being drawn into a holy place
    As I look it's him; were face to face

With tears running down, I sing holy
    My heart for him solely

Invoking his beauty, I lay at his feet
    The fire of God, burning as heat

Embraced by heavens kiss
    I wake in bliss

Face to face
    As heaven embraced

THIS PLACE...

There's a place I go to every morning
    My minds Christ adoring

A place of presence and peace
    A place called the glory feast

A presence so thick my body feels shock
    My eyes closed; my spirits locked

When he comes I am endowed a boiling pot
    Ready to explode I'm so hot

The fire grows in my soul
    There's manna in my bowl

The living water flows into my being
    As my minds focus is decreeing

I catch a glimpse of his face
    My vision see's through the haste

The energy races as my ears ring
    For all the visitations he wants to bring

I encounter the spirit at a new level
    Increase of anointing God's holy pebble

Revelation lifts the veil
    As my spirit becomes a derail

It embraces heavens kiss
    A sweet fragrance his presence count miss

It's at this secret place where I find
    Jesus so divine

THE CLEAR MESSAGE

I was outside enjoying the cool breeze
    When in my spirit screams made me freeze

It was hot and it was dark
    All I could see where souls with a red mark

I could feel the terror and the fear
    I could see the flames of hell in the mirror

God only let me see the reflection
    Of that dungeon; for my protection

The chains in the prison walls
    And the pain felt walking down the halls

I seen souls trying to escape this place
    As demons laughed & spit in there face

The lake of fire these souls soaked in
    I could feel satan's anger as I seen his grin

The hate he has for me and you
    There's no end to what he will do

But the gospel of Jesus Christ lives
    And the freedom his blood gives

The atoning sacrifice saves
    As he rose from the grave

There's a choice life or death
    Where will you go at your last breathe

You don't have to go into the flames
    You can be saved by just one name

His reaching down his love to you
    Please accept this message so true

Don't be blind and lied to no more
    Jesus died to shut the door

As forgiveness and turn sin away
    And be saved this very day

OTHER BOOKS BY TAMMY HENSON

Cries of the Soul

Cries of the Soul
(Volume 2)

www.ingramcontent.com/pod-product-compliance
Lightning Source LLC
Chambersburg PA
CBHW050045080526
44586CB00014B/1463

sought to claim the land and win the hearts of Texas' native inhabitants, the Indians. Decades later, the ingenuity, wit and survival skills of my road's American settlers brought transformation and civilization to this untamed land. And I'll never forget the sincerity and dedication of the early missionaries of many faiths who brought religion to Texas. I've witnessed triumph and tragedy, justice and heinous crime, laughter and tears, success and failure, humility and arrogance, unselfishness and greed. The good mostly outweighed the bad, I'm happy to say. I suppose there's hardly a language or dialect I haven't heard, from the Indians of many tribes to the myriad of nationalities who came. I claim them all as "my people."

As the most ancient of trails, and the earliest land-route through the heart of Texas, I have been called by many names: Old Spanish Trail, San Antonio Road, and The King's Highway. Some have given me more grandiose titles: Great Strategic Military Highway, Road of Manifest Destiny, and Doomed Road of Empire. I am especially pleased with my newest and most descriptive name: *El Camino Real de los Tejas National Historic Trail*. It is best, and I wear it with pride.

PART I
The 2007 Original Edition

Typical Caddo Indian village lifestyle, inclding ceremonial mound
Sketch by Richard Murphy

Chapter One

From the Sabine to the Trinity:
The Caddo Confederacies of East Texas

"In the beginning Texas belonged to God and the Indians..."
Bill Lytch

To Texas residents fortunate enough to live in the eastern half of the State it comes as no surprise that a preponderance of the early Indian tribes chose this section as their home. They were the Caddoes, composed of three rather loosely connected confederacies located throughout all of East Texas, from the Gulf of Mexico to the Red River. The largest of the three was the Hasinai, whose eight tribes lived along the upper Neches and Angelina Rivers. The other two were the Kadohadachos, located around the Red River, and the Natchitoches, who lived in the vicinity of present-day Natchitoches, Louisiana. In addition, three independent Caddo tribes were the Yatasi, the Adais and the Ais (Eyeish, or Hais.) The Caddo confederacies spoke a common language, appropriately called "Caddo," and seemed to live in harmony with one another.

For centuries before the arrival of the intruders the Caddoes lived an idyllic lifestyle, cultivating their crops in virgin soil and hunting plentiful game in untouched, primeval forests. Their villages were located along rivers, streams and bayous, linked together with a well organized system of trails. With abundant rainfall and a cornucopia of edible native plants available at various times of year, the East Texas locale was a veritable Garden of Eden. Their environment protected them with impenetrable forests and a rugged countryside. In return, the Caddoes were conservators of nature, the environmentalists of their time, taking only what was needed for survival and leaving all else undisturbed. It is no wonder that this untouched paradise, as described in the diaries of arriving intruders in the eighteenth and nineteenth centuries, was so appealing...it was the land everyone wanted to possess.

During the process of researching various sources for this book, it was our good fortune to meet Lila Kerr, an undergraduate student at Stephen F. Austin State University. Kerr authored a comprehensive study on "The Caddo Indian

Mounds" which she presented to the fall meeting of the East Texas Historical Association in 2005. It is refreshing to discover a talented young person who realizes the importance of recording, preserving, and promoting history. Selected excerpts from Kerr's paper provide insights into the lifestyle, culture, and customs of the Caddo Indians, whose trails formed the basis for much of *El Camino Real* in East Texas.

Caddo Lifestyle and Culture

"Caddo means 'pierced nose.' The Caddo Indians practiced tatooing and piercing. Men often wore ornaments through their noses. Men and women often painted themselves with bright colors and wore shells, bones, animal teeth, seeds, and feathers as ornaments. The women parted, oiled and plaited their hair into one braid and wore sleeveless buckskin blouses with skirts fringed along the hem with metal trinkets and seeds tied to it. In the winter, they wore fur capes to keep themselves warm. The Nacogdoches Indians have been referred to as the 'white Indians.' Father Solis (1727) described the Nacogdoches Indian women as being 'white with disheveled yellow hair.' According to a Spanish explorer and his crew who spent a full winter with them because of snow, they were a friendly and hospitable type of people. The Caddo Indians have been considered the most civilized Indians in prehistoric times.

"Caddo villages often contained 800 to 2000 people living in them. The homes and villages were permanent and normally located near a stream, which helped them when growing their crops. Many archaeologists believe that the reason the Caddo Indians settled in the Nacogdoches area was the protecting hills which provided lookout posts for sentries, necessary water supplies such as LaNana and Banita Creeks, an ample food supply in a concentrated area, and a peaceful, comfortable lifestyle in a mild climate. In contrast, some other Indian tribes had to travel over a wide area to obtain food and withstood harsh weather conditions at certain times of year. Their homes were conical structures made by lashing organic materials to a wooden frame. Normally fifteen to twenty poles were placed in a circle in the ground and then tops of them were lassoed together with wet leather straps. An escape hole was left at the top of the hut for smoke, from a fire burned in the middle of the floor space, to escape. Next, the roof and sides were thatched with straw and cornstalks. One home could be built in a morning when the whole community pitched in. The family who was going to live in the hut provided corn and meat for the workers when they were finished. These homes often lasted for thirty to forty years. The interior of the hut contained two levels of overhead storage shelves and a drying rack in the upper part of the structure which also served as work platforms during construction. Elevated beds ringed the perimeter of the hut, reserved for any village leader who might need sleeping space during a visit. A small fire was burned continually on the hearth to provide warmth, keep the interior and all of the stored goods dry, and discourage insects from nesting in the cane. If it was accidentally extinguished, it was re-lighted from the temple mound fire which was never allowed to die. The huts were also weatherproof, keeping the interior warm in the winter and cool in the summer. One hut normally housed ten to twelve people. The Caddos received their food from a variety of places. One way was through farming. The main crops they planted were squash, pumpkins, maize, corn, beans, potatoes, melons, and tobacco. They saved two years worth of corn in case of a fire or drought. The community had to work together in order to plant enough food to feed the hundreds of people living there. They also developed a crop rotation method to use for farming, which is still used today by farmers. Their method was planting different crops each year in the same soil. Another way of getting food was by hunting. They trapped rabbits, coyotes, foxes, and beavers in pits they dug and baited. They used dogs to hunt animals and made the dog carry their catch on a travois, a V-shaped sled made of saplings. They also used the trotline method to catch fish. A long heavy fishing line was stretched across a creek with several baited hooks on it and weights to keep it underwater. Another way of getting food was by gathering it. They gathered wild berries, nuts, figs, peaches, and honey.

"The Caddos had many pastime activities. They were famous for the pottery they made from clay and often traded it with the Plains Indians for other goods. The Caddo Indians were believed to have a wide range of trading connections, including in the Circum-Caribbean area. They also made mats, sieves, traps, and baskets from bamboo canes. They made water jugs by lining a basket with clay and carried loads on their backs connected to a trumpline. A trumpline was like a headband that circled the forehead. This helped balance the weight of the load. Sports were another pastime for the Caddos. Many games were used to train young men for war. In a letter to M.B. Lamar, the Caddos were described as the most warlike Indians in Texas but least averse to the art of peace. An example of war training games were foot races which helped build strength and speed. Other games were for fun. They had a game like hockey and a guessing game. The guessing game was played by lining up their moccasins with an object hidden in one of the moccasins. Whoever guessed the moccasin with the object in it was the winner.

"The Caddo Indians' government was fairly simple. Each clan had a council of men and a clan chief who was also a member of the tribal council. Each tribe had a civil chief, who was in charge of tribal affairs, and a war chief. The tribes also had graduated officers with special duties civically and religiously. The leader of a tribe was called a caddi. They gave orders, made decisions, and supervised projects. The position of caddi was normally passed from fathers to sons, but women sometimes became caddi."

Caddo Burial Customs and Temple Mounds

"The Caddo Indian society was split into two classes: the lower class and the elite(higher) class. Normally the mounds were built by the 'common' or lower class. In fact, the labor put into the mounds suggests that there was a well-developed political system that could induce, direct, and organize the populace into fashioning mounds. They carried soil from quarry pits in thirty to forty pound baskets and deposited them on the mounds. Six stages were normally required to complete a mound. Mounds were located mainly in the inner village. The inner village contained two temple mounds and a burial mound.

"The temple mounds had temples or other public buildings built on top of them or near them. They demonstrated the elite group's authority in society. Log faced stairs led from ceremonial courts to the tops of temple mounds. These mounds express a developed technological base and an advanced and well-organized society (probably focused on a religion based on sun worship.) It is believed that the mounds were used for religious ceremonies conducted by priestly castes. The temples were like ordinary dwellings. The temple was furnished with an altar made of mat reeds and various other reed mats. Benches were placed to one side of the door. In front of a bed and raised slightly above ground was a wooden bench which held tobacco, a pipe with feathers, and pottery vessels used to burn fat offerings. In the center of the temple burned a perpetual fire which was fed with four heavy logs pointed in cardinal directions. Temples were attended by Xinesis, the temporal rulers of Caddoans.

"One of the temple mound rituals practiced is illustrated in the *Story of Coconicis*. Near the temple were two small houses belonging to two Coconicis boys whom the Supreme Being had sent to help the Caddos. They served as intermediaries and oracles between the Supreme God and the Xinesi. No one was allowed to see them because it would bring instant death. Occasionally, the Xinesi summoned the tribes of the Confederacy and called into the temple the tribal leaders and elders. Then all lights were extinguished. The Xinesi spoke to the Coconisis, prayed, and when the prayer concluded, threw a gourd rattle on the ground. If the gourd made a sound, it meant that if they kept the promise they had made, everything they had asked for would be given to them. If there was no sound, it meant that God was angry with them. They believed in an omnipotent deity but they also believed that the world was inhabited by multitudes of supernatural powerful creatures.

"The burial mounds were used to bury members of the elite group. Archaeologists know this because of some of the artifacts they have uncovered from some of the mounds. They have found pottery, arrowheads, earspools, and other stone items, like effigy pipes and cells (axeheads.) Stone was a symbol of wealth and status because it was not found in their area and had to be imported. The artifacts that were found in the mounds had been placed there as an offering to the dead in their afterlife. Sometimes multiple burials were found, and this suggested the sacrifice of family members or servants. Members of the chief's staff were killed and buried with him and it was considered an honor to accompany their leader into the afterlife. Murphy said, 'Indians never bury their dead in a flat because they did not have tools to cut through the clay so they buried them above the clay.' The head of the dead always faced the west.

"Through excavations, archaeologists have found that the mounds near Alto, Texas were built during the Early Caddo times and the Nacogdoches mounds were built during the Middle Caddo times. The mounds in Alto had not been well preserved as the land had been plowed and gophers had destroyed part of them. The mounds in Nacogdoches were very well preserved since they had been set aside as public commons and had never been cleared for fields or plowed. SFA sociologists analyzing Caddo relics and artifacts at the Caddo village site on the Rusk Middle School campus estimated the times as 1250 to 1350 A.D. Historians say that when the Europeans arrived in East Texas in the seventeenth century, Indians living here were not sure who had built the mounds but through the artifacts, archaeologists have determined that it was the Caddo Indians who built them.

Fate of the Caddo Indians

"The population of Caddo Indians in the Nacogdoches area might have reached 1,000 before beginning to decline. The Caddos were not as warlike as the Apache and Comanche. Therefore, when Europeans came to the area, the Caddos did not try to fight them. First came the hunters on horseback. This was a problem for the Indians because they could not get enough horses to compete with the hunters. Next came the Spanish, who tried to establish a mission. *Mission Nuestra Senora de Guadalupe de los Nacogdoches* was established to convert the Indians and to have a Spanish hold in Texas. Mission life for the Indians contained a daily schedule of learning religious studies and trades. However, many of the Indians were sickened by disease and others ran away because they did not like life in the missions. Next came the white European settlers moving to Texas and wanting to build on Caddo lands. Though disease killed many of the Indians, many were forced to move to Oklahoma, where they remain now.

"In conclusion, the Caddo Indians were the most successful among prehistoric groups in the late eighth century A.D. in the East Texas area. They remained an important part in the history of this area until 1700 A.D. Much information about their lifestyle and culture, burial and temple mounds, and fate has been revealed through the study of Caddoan mounds in East Texas. Though the Caddos no longer live in Nacogdoches, the residents of this community are reminded of them each time they say the name of their town or see the historical marker on Mound Street." [1]

It is interesting to East Texans that our state name was derived from the Caddoes of our area, the Hasinai Confederation. The Hasinai tribes greeted each other with the word *Tayshas*, (or *Tehas*) meaning "allies" or "friends." When Father Massanet arrived with the Spaniards in 1690 a Caddo Chief met him with the same *"Tehas"* greeting. The Father determined that this word used so frequently in the Caddo culture was an appropriate means of describing the unknown land in which these friendly peoples lived.

Centuries later, Texas citizens still take pride in being "The Friendship State."

Garden, Grass House, and Museum at Caddo Mounds State Historic Site
Photograph provided by Rachel Galan

Typical East Texas mission scene photograph of exhibit in
Mission Dolores State Historic Site
Used by permission

Chapter Two

Signs of the Cross and Sword:
The East Texas Missions and Presidios

Father Damien Massanet, the priest who accompanied Alonso de Leon on several expeditions from Mexico in 1689-90, was impressed with the friendliness displayed by the Caddo tribes, and felt they were ripe for conversion to the Catholic faith. As a result, the first mission in Texas was built in 1690, *Francisco de los Tejas* in present-day Houston County. Establishing additional missions seemed a good idea to both Massanet and De Leon, since the original purpose of their expeditions was to investigate the Frenchman LaSalle's alarming intrusion into territory already claimed by Spain. Even more disturbing was the discovery that the French were crossing the Sabine and trading with the East Texas Indians on a regular basis. Several well-placed missions could serve a two-fold purpose: convert the native tribes and, at the same time, provide barriers to French encroachment.

When he made his report concerning these expeditions, Father Massanet called the land *Tayshas,* or *Tehas,* the term used in the everyday language of the Caddoes. When this report was conveyed to the King's Council in Spain immediate action was taken.

In 1691, the Junta from the Crown of Spain officially named the land *"Texas."* In this edict "Three purposes were stated: First, *Don Domingo Teran de los Rios* was appointed the first governor of the Province of the Hasinai Indians and adjacent regions, and Monclova was the Capitol. Second, Governor Teran was ordered to find a new land route, a straight line direct from Monclova to the Eastern Indians, as traveled by Father Massanet and De Leon in 1690 when building the first mission, *Francisco de los Tejas,* abandoning the indirect and circuitous route by way of the Gulf." Along this road missions were to be established east of the Trinity, and one near Natchitoches, Louisiana to guard against the French. "Third, the watch was set for the rank and file of the world. Toll was required to travel and carry a burden from Mexico to *Adaes Mission.*

"Governor Teran was advised to keep a diary noting and naming all the rivers, observing the character of the natives and describing the products of the country. He was advised to continue the policy of courting the friendship and good will of the Indians, and observe their wishes in choosing sites for the proposed missions."[2]

A second East Texas mission was founded in late 1690, Santisimo Nombre de Maria, located on the Neches River about five miles east of the *San Francisco de los Tejas Mission.*

By the time Teran arrived in the area in 1691 both of these early missions were already failing. Besides, the French threat no longer seemed urgent. The two missions were abandoned completely by 1693, and the province of Texas was virtually forgotten by the Spaniards for the next twenty years.

Father Francisco Hidalgo, one of the six original priests involved in the planning stages of *Mission Tejas* in 1690, still held to the dream of re-establishing the East Texas missions. His entreaties to the Spanish crown for the implementation of his goal went unanswered for nearly two decades. By 1711 Father Hidalgo had devised another plan. He wrote a rather unusual letter to the French Governor in Louisiana, Sieur de Cadillac, asking him to assist in the establishment of Spanish missions in East Texas. Surprisingly, this proposal was met with a positive response. Governor Cadillac had been charged with operating the French colony in a profitable manner, but prior attempts at establishing a trade relationship with Spain had failed. Helping Father Hidalgo with his religious endeavors provided the perfect opportunity, or excuse, to enter Texas via the Sabine River, a frontier hundreds of miles away from the Spanish authorities in Mexico, where, perhaps, regulations governing international trade were not strictly enforced. Governor Cadillac chose an adventuresome, charismatic young Frenchman named St. Denis to lead the expedition into Texas in 1714.

St. Denis had already begun making a name for himself by founding Natchitoches, Louisiana in 1713, and building Post St. Jean Baptiste in 1714. He was charged with traveling from the Sabine to the Rio Grande by way of the overland route, a feat he accomplished in six weeks without being stopped or particularly noticed at any point along the way. Since his earlier travels in Louisiana and around the Red River had brought him in contact with Caddo tribes, St. Denis had no trouble relating to them on his journey along King's Highway. His arrival at the Presidio San Juan Bautista Del Rio Grande de Norte in the state of Coahuila, Mexico was cause for alarm among the Mexican authorities. They remembered LaSalle, and suspected French intrusion once again. St. Denis was informed that foreign traders were not permitted to enter

Spanish territory by order of the Crown. He was adamant: his expedition was purely for developing a highway for trade along the logical overland route, *El Camino Real*. Besides, he had searched for Father Hidalgo throughout the entire journey. He reported that the East Texas Indians fervently longed for the return of the missionaries to their region.

Major Diego Ramon, Commander of the Presidio, placed St. Denis under light "house arrest," awaiting instructions from Mexico City as to what to do with him. As the days passed amid a measure of freedom, St. Denis met the captivating step-granddaughter of Major Ramon. Ever the charming Frenchman, St. Denis initiated a courtship with the beautiful young girl, and a promise of marriage soon followed. Louis Juchereau de St. Denis and Dona Maria Manuela Sanchez were married on February 17, 1716 in the Chapel of the Presidio.

By July of 1716, the resourceful St. Denis had convinced Spanish authorities in Mexico City of his trustworthiness, and he was set free. Their opinion of him was so favorable that he was selected to join the Ramon Expedition as commissary officer and guide. The expedition's vital purpose was to re-establish Spanish missions in Eastern Texas in such numbers that French encroachment would be thwarted. Presidios would be established to provide military protection for the missions. Leader of the expedition was Captain Domingo Ramon, Major Ramon's son. Another son, Diego Ramon II, went along as well. Bidding Manuela a tender farewell, and entrusting her to the safekeeping of Major Ramon, St. Denis and the expedition of seventy-five persons departed for East Texas via *El Camino Real*.

In 1716 and 1717, St. Denis participated in the founding of five missions in Eastern Texas, and a mission in Western Louisiana. 'St. Denis played an active part in establishing Spanish presence in East Texas, and his skill in Indian relations and willing cooperation with the padres made a favorable impression on them."[3]

The 1690 mission, *San Francisco de los Tejas*, was revived, and the name changed to *San Francisco de los Neches*. It was moved to a new site further inland on the Neches River near the present city of Alto. A grateful Father Hidalgo accepted the appointment as priest of the restored mission. The other missions, their founding dates and approximate locations, were as follows: *Mission Nuestra Senora de Guadalupe de los Nacogdoches,* 1716, in the present city of Nacogdoches; *Mission Nuestra Senora de la Purisima Conception*, 1716, near the Linwood crossing of the Angelina River; *Mission*

San Jose de los Nazonis, 1716, on one of the tributaries of Shawnee Creek, near the present town of Cushing and the northern line of Nacogdoches County; *Mission Nuestra Senora de los Dolores de los Ais,* 1717, in the present city of San Augustine; and *Mission San Miguel de los Adaes,* 1717, near Robeline, Louisiana.

A presidio, or garrison, was established by Captain Ramon in 1716. Located east of the Trinity River just south of the *San Francisco de los Neches Mission, Presidio Nuestra Senora de los Dolores* (or *Tejas*) was to provide military protection for all of the East Texas missions.

After the founding of the first four missions, Father Antonio Margil de Jesus joined his companions the following year, 1717, establishing *Mission Dolores de los Ais* and ministering throughout the East Texas mission field. In 1992, an article in the Nacogdoches Sampler written by SFA's Dr. Francis Edward Abernethy described Father Margil as "a knotted cord of a man, slim of build but powerful and with the endurance of a Spanish mule." Dr. Abernethy's story continued:

> "In the summer of 1718...the scattered waterholes in La Nana Creek and La Banita finally disappeared, and the cicada sang over dry creek beds...In the extremity Father Margil went to...a high bank where La Nana made a sharp bend, and he knelt and prayed. He prayed for the Nacogdoches Indians and for the missionaries that had come so far and accomplished so little, and he prayed for the parched and dying land...Then, when the sun became round the next morning, he arose and touched the bank with his staff, twice. Two springs of living water sprang forth. They would be called *Los Ojos de Padre Margil.* Because *Los Ojos* means both "eyes" and "springs," these later were called both the Eyes and the Springs of Father Margil. The people of the village were jubilant. They came all day, drinking and filling their pots from the springs, and this blessing was never exhausted." [4]

Dr. Abernethy began looking for the lost springs in 1985 while working on the La Nana Creek Trail. By early 1992 what seemed to be the original twin springs had been uncovered in an area on La Nana Creek fitting the description given by numerous persons who remembered their location.

By 1719 conditions at all six missions and the presidio had deteriorated to such a low level that closure seemed inevitable. To make matters worse,

Nacogdoches LaNana Creek gathering of priests, soldiers, and Native Americans *Archival image*

the poorly defended *Los Adaes Mission* had been attacked by French soldiers from the nearby fort at Natchitoches. While the victors were stealing chickens from the mission's chicken house, the lone lay brother was able to escape across the Sabine to *Mission Dolores de los Ais* and Father Margil, where he reported "The Chicken War." All six missions and the presidio were abandoned immediately, unaware that a royal decree had been issued in mid-1718 to strengthen the missions in East Texas by placing military guards at each one.

The appointment of The Marques de Aguayo as the new governor of Coahuila and Texas was both timely and financially prudent for the Crown. Aguayo's heritage was that of distinguished Spanish knights and noblemen, but his best asset was his wife Ignacia, a woman of tremendous wealth and land holdings in Coahuila. Governor Aguayo's proposal to Spanish authorities for an expedition into Texas was one that they could not refuse: at his own personal expense, he would rid the province of the bothersome French once and for all, and he would re-establish the six deserted missions.

On March 24, 1721, Aguayo's expedition left Mexico. He "had assembled five hundred men, tons of supplies, and thousands of head of livestock...The large numbers of stock made this the first big 'cattle' drive in Texas history. Aguayo had acquired twenty-eight hundred horses, forty-eight hundred cattle, and sixty-four hundred sheep and goats... Spanish ranching in Texas truly began with the arrival of these huge herds in 1721.",$_5$

As might be imagined, an entourage of this magnitude would certainly have transformed the already existing *El Camino Real* into a well-trodden thoroughfare. Aguayo & Company followed the historic trace to the former mission sites, taking care at each location to rebuild, restore and make safe the settlement. The decision was made to move the old *Presidio Dolores* (or *Presidio de los Tejas*) from the Neches River to a site close to the Angelina River. Across the Sabine River, *Mission San Miguel de Linares de Los Adaes* was re-established at a new site, but still in the vicinity of present-day Robeline, Louisiana.

About a half-mile from the *Adaes Mission* Governor Aguayo established the *Presidio of Nuestra Senora del Pilar de los Adaes*, and staffed it with a hundred Spanish cavalrymen, thirty-one of whom brought their families. Salaries were 450 pesos a year, payable in goods, not money. According to Cornial Cox, Interpretive Ranger at the *Presidio Adaes* site, there were thirteen buildings inside the perimeter of the presidio, and six cannons. The surrounding pine-post palisade was ten to twelve feet high. Ranger Cox has

Los Adaes marker near Robeline, Louisana

constructed an outline form of the presidio on the rolling hillside behind the Visitor's Center at *Los Adaes* Park. Faint traces of the old *El Camino Real* wagon trail on the north side of the presidio are still visible. On the day we visited the park, Cox was dressed in the traditional Spanish soldier's uniform, which included leather knee pants and leggings, a bloused shirt, and black silk scarves for both head and neck. He frequently brandished his sword, gesturing toward the various points of interest. Engaged in a running narration, he spoke of the meaning of the Caddo word, *"Adaes,"* which means "Those people who live over in the woods." Upon our return to the modern Visitor's Center and small museum, Ranger Cox was gracious enough to draw a map showing the directions to Rio Hondo, the easternmost boundary of No Man's Land.

Governor Aguayo's establishment of *Presidio Adaes* was for the protection of Spanish interests on both sides of the Sabine River. However, Natchitoches and Post St. Jean Baptiste, only fifteen miles away from the presidio and mission, were a little too close for comfort. Aguayo wanted assurances that the French would stay on their side of the Rio Hondo, the recognized boundary line between Spanish Texas and French Louisiana. On August 1, 1721 he met with the Commandant of Post St. Jean Baptiste (our dashing young friend St. Denis) with the demand that the French stay out of Texas. St. Denis took one look at the commanding size of Aguayo's forces, and realized he had no choice but to comply.

St. Denis had returned to Natchitoches in 1719 after another brush with the Spanish authorities. He was appointed Commandant of the French Post in 1720, a position he held for twenty-four years. By 1721 Spanish officials allowed his wife, the lovely Manuela, to join him in Natchitoches. St. Denis died in 1744. He was survived by Manuela and seven children. When Manuela died in 1758, she was buried next to her husband near Post St. Jean Baptiste. "The annals of Natchitoches record that she was the wealthiest woman in Louisiana. Northwestern State University of Louisiana now occupies the property of her estate." [6]

"In 1729, Spain designated *Los Adaes* the capital of the province of Texas. This made *Los Adaes* the official residence of the governor, and a house was constructed for him within the presidio. *Los Adaes* remained the administrative seat of Government for the entire province for the next forty-four years." [7]

The mission era ended in East Texas with the Spanish King's 1771 decree entitled "New Regulations for Presidios." The royal edict was issued a few years after the Marquis de Rubi visited Texas on an inspection tour of the missions and presidios. Rubi had traveled from San Antonio to Los Adaes in 1767, and had nothing but the harshest of criticism for his findings. His advice: abandon all missions and presidios in Texas except those located in San Antonio and La Bahia. By 1773 the post at Los Adaes was closed, and all the inhabitants (estimated at between 300 and 500) were required to relocate in San Antonio, the newly designated capital of the Texas province.

The question may be asked, "How is it that Spain claimed title to Texas centuries before the arrival of any other nation?" The answer lies in the Treaty of Tordesilles made between Portugal and Spain in 1494. Simply put, Spain was awarded all land discovered at that time or thereafter in the half-portion of the hemisphere that included North America and most of South America, while Portugal received the other half. Thus, beginning with the explorer Pineda in 1519, "the Spaniards had continued to penetrate the unknown land from all points of the compass"...searching for fabulous rich kingdoms...and later, solidifying their permanent presence in Texas through a spirit of missionary zeal and the establishment of missions throughout the province. [8]

Cornial Cox, Interpretive Ranger at the *Los Adaes Mission* near Robeline, Louisana. The mission was founded in 1717 for Adaes Indians by Fra Margil, Franciscan of Zacatecas, who traversed the trail from Panama on foot. French Natchitoches was served by missionaries from this easternmost Spanish post.

Part of the ancient trail just off of Lousiana Highway 6,
an extension of Texas Highway 21, near Los Adaes

Old Stone Fort located on campus of Stephen F. Austin State University, Nacogdoches, TX
Sketch by Richard Murphy

Chapter Three

Gil Y'Barbo: His Legacy Lives On

An impressive bronze statue of Antonio Gil Y'Barbo stands on the east side of Plaza Principal in downtown Nacogdoches, a permanent reminder of the heroic Spanish Texan whose life left an imprint throughout the entire East Texas region. Gil Y'Barbo is appropriately recognized as the Father of Nacogdoches, for he reclaimed the settlement's choice location in 1779, and established a firm foundation of strong leadership that allowed the village to grow and thrive.

Gil Y'Barbo's sphere of influence went much farther than the immediate Nacogdoches area. It spread up and down *El Camino Real*, from *Los Adaes* to the Trinity River. He enters our story in 1772, when the East Texas missions and presidios were finally closed for good.

Y'Barbo's parents were married in 1723 at the Alamo Mission Church in San Antonio. His father, Matheo Antonio Y'Barbo, a Spanish soldier, was a native of Andalucia, Spain. His mother, Juana Luzgarda Hernandez, was most likely from that area as well. Matheo was assigned to *Presidio Nuestra del Pilar de los Adaes*, where Gil Antonio was born in 1729. The intelligent young lad was exposed to Spanish, French and Indian cultures as he grew. A familiarity with the diverse lifestyles represented in the *Los Adaes* area served him well in future years in his relationships with all types of people. His adeptness and skill in dealing with the Indian tribes was legendary.

Y'Barbo learned the easy, interactive system of trade already well established in the East Texas area. The Spanish Crown had forbidden trade with other nations, particularly the French, and the colonists were not to trade with the Indians on an individual basis. The Spanish authorities who were expected to enforce these stringent rules and regulations were too far away to be effective, so both legal and illicit trading were in full swing as Gil grew to manhood. Gil developed an excellent reputation as a trader, albeit at times "smuggler" would have been a more descriptive word. Expediency was the order of the day.

When Gil's parents moved to *Los Adaes* in the 1720s their friends, the Pedro Padilla family, moved with them, settling in the area around the Nacogdoches mission. Around 1749 Gil married Maria Padilla, Pedro's daughter. The couple established their home and ranch, *El Lobanillo*, located along *El Camino Real* in present-day Geneva, Texas, about fifteen miles from the *Dolores de los Ais Mission*. Translation of the title *El Lobanillo* was "wart" or "mole"... a term which expressed the opinion of several Spanish officials concerning the worrisome clandestine trade being conducted from its location. Gil and Maria were parents to four children, Mariano, Marcos, Maria Antonia, and Maria Josefa.

As the end of the French and Indian War drew near in 1762, France ceded Louisiana and its possessions west of the Mississippi River to Spain to prevent a take-over by Great Britain. With all of Louisiana under Spanish control there was no further need for the frontier-guarding outpost and mission east of the Sabine River. The closing paragraphs of Chapter Two relate the Crown's decision to move all inhabitants of the missions and presidios to San Antonio, the new capitol of the Texas province.

In 1773, the unpleasant task of enforcing the Imperial Decree was assigned to the new governor of the province, Juan Maria Baron de Ripperda. In office since 1769, Ripperda liked the East Texas settlers, especially Gil Y'Barbo, the talented trader who had gained his confidence by assisting him in securing needed goods and supplies. Governor Ripperda was sympathetic to the plight of the settlers, but had no choice except to comply. The Adaesanos had only a few days to gather families and belongings, and leave their established homes in the East Texas area. They left unharvested crops in the fields and stray farm animals in the pine forest. Thus began their sad, three-month trek to San Antonio.

From the journey's outset Antonio Gil Y'Barbo was the acknowledged leader of the nearly five hundred travelers. At *El Lobanillo* he left his mother, other relatives and those too ill to continue–about two dozen persons–in the care of his son, certainly indicating that he did not consider this forced evacuation permanent. About that same number of the group remained in the Nacogdoches area. The rest of the evacuees pushed on toward San Antonio down *El Camino Real*, a trip so excruciating that ten children died along the way. Another thirty Adaesanos died after arriving in San Antonio, their health broken as a result of the harsh journey. To make matters worse, all the prime tracts were already taken; the displaced East Texans were outcasts in an unfamiliar land.

Gil Y'Barbo authored a petition asking Governor Ripperda for permission to return to East Texas. Since a reversal of the royal edict could only be given in Mexico City, Y'Barbo and his friend Gil Flores offered to carry the request to Viceroy Antonio Maria de Bucareli. The answer was "Yes, you may settle anywhere between the Trinity and Sabine." Unfortunately, Hugo Oconer, a proven enemy of both Governor Ripperda and Gil Y'Barbo, made an untimely entrance into the picture with dire admonitions that illicit trade must not be allowed to begin again; the rules must be strictly enforced. In an effort to maintain harmony, Viceroy Bucareli agreed to a compromise: "No, you may not return to *Los Adaes*, but East Texas further inland is permitted, with Governor Ripperda selecting the site." The settlers joyously left San Antonio, declaring Gil Y'Barbo their hero: "the restorer of his country, lover of the common good, and father of the Adaesanos."[9]

Ripperda chose a location on the Trinity River for the displaced Adaesanos. By early 1775 the settlers reached their new destination. Gil named the settlement Nuestra Senora de Pilar de Bucareli, in honor of the Viceroy. With this new lease on life, the nearly 350 residents built homes and reestablished their lives at Bucareli. Y'Barbo received the title of Captain and Mayor, with Gil Flores designated as Lieutenant. After four years of a relatively peaceful existence, Bucareli was attacked several times by Comanche Indians, the Trinity River flooded the townsite, and some of the settlers began drifting back toward the east. Soon afterward half the buildings caught fire and burned. This was the last straw. Gil gathered his remaining people, sent word to San Antonio of his planned departure, and headed east on the *Camino Real* in late January 1779. By March or April 1779 Gil Y'Barbo and his followers had established a permanent settlement in Nacogdoches alongside *El Camino Real*, where a remnant of the old mission still remained. Father Jose Francisco de la Garza was in residence as priest.

Y'Barbo petitioned the Spanish government "for reimbursement of funds expended from his private fortune. Don Antonio contended that he and his son had spent thousands of pesos on the aid and protection of East Texas settlers...he requested arms to defend Nacogdoches, which did not have a presidio." By October 1779 the government had awarded Y'Barbo an annual salary of 500 pesos, with joint titles of lieutenant governor, chief justice of Nacogdoches, and captain of militia. Soon afterward he received appointment as "judge of contraband seizures."[10]

Always on good terms with the Indians, and cognizant of the need to provide sustenance for the settlers, Y'Barbo received permission to establish a trading post, or commissary, in Nacogdoches. A large two-story stone house, circa 1778 or 1779, was his headquarters. We know it today as the historic Old Stone Fort, one of the oldest and most impressive Spanish structures in Texas. Moved from its original location facing *Camino Real*, it has been carefully reconstructed and preserved on the campus of Stephen F. Austin State University.

Of course, there is much more to the intriguing story of Gil Antonio Y'Barbo. Suffice it to say that this stalwart Spaniard ruled Nacogdoches with a firm hand for more than twelve years. His lengthy Criminal Code, published in Nacogdoches in 1783, were found in the Nacogdoches Archives and translated by historian and court reporter R.B. Blake during the 1930s. The Code listed possible crimes and their resulting punishments in graphic detail, for the purpose of informing the "ignorant and evil-disposed." One cannot imagine committing any of the listed sins with the possibility, for example, of being "hanged after being quartered alive." Given the hardships and lawless environment of these primitive times, Chief Justice Y'Barbo must have considered drastic consequences necessary in order to properly enforce the Code.

There is no doubt, however, that Gil Y'Barbo had the best interests of his settlers at heart during his tenure as their leader. Even Father Margil and Father Hidalgo did not frown on his commercial ventures in regard to trade. The importance of his efforts in helping the settlers return to East Texas, his constant care and protection of them upon their return, and his skillful assistance in re-establishing their lives during the earliest days of the Texas frontier cannot be emphasized enough. In 1787 Father Garza, the Nacogdoches missionary, expressed the feelings of the East Texans toward Gil Y'Barbo: he was "the father, protector, and comforter of their recovered homeland."[11]

In 1809 Gil Y'Barbo was eighty years old. He was long retired, and had established a home, Rancho La Lucana, on the west bank of the Attoyac River, near King's Highway. When he died that year, he was buried in the Old Spanish Cemetery, a location now under the present Nacogdoches County Courthouse.

*

Our research concerning Antonio Gil Y'Barbo precipitated a visit to his direct descendant Hubert Y'Barbo, who lives near Chireno, Texas in Nacogdoches County. Hubert and his wife Alice have built their home on a large acreage of family land down the road from Our Lady of Lourdes Catholic Church and Cemetery, just off *El Camino Real*.

We spent several hours with this amicable couple as they recalled interesting details about Hubert's famous ancestor. Alice Y'Barbo is a genealogist and historian of the first order. Thoroughly familiar with her subject, she recounted in rapid-fire succession the seven generations from Gil to Hubert, with interesting details in between. Hubert's line came from Gil's eldest son Mariano, to Waldo Pedro, to Jose Luciano, to Vital Victor, to Robert, and to Hubert. Interestingly, Hubert is also a direct descendant of Jose Antonio Chireno, for whom the nearby town of Chireno was named. His two grandfathers were Vidal Victor Y'Barbo, and John Falcon from the Chireno line.

Hubert Y'Barbo, direct descendant of Gil Y'Barbo and José Antonio Chireno

Typical Ferry on Sabine River at James Gaines Crossing
Sketch by Richard Murphy

Chapter Four

Ferry Tales

Exiting the dense forest and the umbrage of mammoth trees that grow along western Louisiana's Highway 6, the present-day traveler is greeted by an entirely diverse vista...the Pendleton Bridge spanning the awe-inspiring expanse of water known as Toledo Bend Reservoir. It is almost as if a curtain is drawn back exposing a new world of sea birds, cresting waves, sandy beaches, and an expansive sky of rolling clouds and spectacular sunsets.

It seems incongruous that this very spot was the site of the ferry at the *El Camino Real* crossing, where a primitive wooden flat-boat transported early settlers across the Sabine River into Texas country. At that time the Sabine was a snag-strewn, muddy river whose current was subject at all times to the wiles of nature...calm and placid in the summer season, often angry and unpredictable in the winter months. In the early 1800's her banks were covered with moss-shrouded oaks, willows, beech, and huge cypress trees reaching ever upward in their quest to reach the sky. The name Sabine...*Rio de Sabinas*... is derived from the Spanish word meaning "cypress." Apparently Domingo Ramon named the river during his mission-establishing expedition in 1716, because it is so named on maps as early as 1721.

We were fortunate to have as our primary source of information on the Sabine River's early ferries the late Joy Shealy of Nacogdoches, who generously shared her extensive research and maps with us. Joy's interest in the history of East Texas increased when she and her husband purchased property on Toledo Bend Reservoir in 1982. She had time and opportunity to explore the original sites along *El Camino Real*, and travel the rural "back roads" in her quest for little known, previously undocumented facts concerning land lines, grants and early settlers. In the process of her genealogical research Joy learned that she was a descendant of James Gaines, a finding that increased her interest in the ferries. After moving to Nacogdoches in 2003, Joy continued her research endeavors and interviews with the assistance of Connie Hodges. There were several ferries located along the Sabine River near *El Camino Real,* the earliest being the Crow Ferry in 1794, established by Isaac (or Michael) Crow. It was purchased by Bradford Carter in the 1850's, and later owned by Burrell Thompson. Joy Shealy called it Thompson's Ferry. According to longtime Sabine County residents, the Carter Ferry Road is perhaps the oldest of the

Camino Reales, where evidence of an interesting Indian campground is still visible beside the road.

Other ferries were Patterson's Ferry, also known as the upper crossing, and the Chambers Ferry, where a buoy in Toledo Bend Lake marks the location near the present Braggtown settlement on the Texas side. Gerald Stewart, whose childhood was spent in the Braggtown area, vividly remembers fishing in the Sabine while seated on the remains of one of the old ferries. Burr's Ferry was established south of the present Toledo Bend Bridge.

Another crossing remembered was an old Indian ford called *Los Ormigas,* later named East Hamilton when Sam Houston, Philip Sublett, A.G. Kellogg and William Kerr laid out and incorporated the town in 1839. The first U.S. Post Office in Texas was opened at East Hamilton on March 8, 1847. Growing along the bank of the Sabine River at East Hamilton was an immense cypress tree, a sentinel of the forest thought to be over one thousand years old. This majestic tree exceeded thirty-four feet in circumference. It was named the Sam Houston Cypress in his honor. Tragically, the waters of Toledo Bend Reservoir have covered its massive canopy, its stately presence lost forever. Today, East Hamilton is a ghost town.

There were several places along the Sabine that could be crossed without using the ferries, especially during the summer months. Joy Shealy located one such spot about a mile above Patterson's Ferry called "The Salt Flats, where the water was so shallow at times that the Indians, Spanish and Mexicans could walk across." There was also the Moran Crossing, not far from the present Bragg Chapel Church, where one could easily wade from the Texas side

The enigmatic caves on Toledo Bend Reservoir,
a portion of the mystique still lingers

to the Louisiana side when the Sabine was low. Judy Hodges' father, a Braggtown resident, visited her mother in this fashion during their courtship. All along the shrouded twists and turns of the River before it became a Reservoir mysterious tales abounded of pirate caves and buried treasure... lead mines and Spanish coins...and relics of both Indians and early pioneers long since gone.

The most intriguing of all the Ferry Tales centers around the Gaines, or Pendleton Ferry. This ferry site was originally established by Louis Sharbeno (Chabineaux, Charbanon) in 1797. He and his wife Margaret operated the ferry until tragedy struck in 1801. As the ferry barge crossed the Sabine a spirited horse belonging to one of the passengers kicked Sharbeno overboard into the River, an unfortunate event which resulted in his drowning. Upon hearing the sad news, Isaac (or Michael) Crow set out to comfort the widow at her home. A romance ensued, and marriage soon followed. Crow and Margaret continued to operate the ferry at the present-day *El Camino Real* location.

Margaret's daughter, Mary Sharbeno, met privateer James Campbell in 1814 while visiting in Natchitoches, Louisiana. Campbell had enlisted in the United States Navy in 1812 as a sailmaker, but was serving as gunner on the USS Constitution when the British frigate Guerriere's mast was destroyed. This victory over the British Navy won the US ship the nickname of "Old Ironsides," resulting in the patriotic poem by the same name penned by Oliver Wendell Holmes. In 1813 Campbell was assigned as sail maker for Commodore Oliver Hazard Perry, and helped engage the British Fleet during the Battle of Lake Erie. His naval term of service over, Campbell sailed to New Orleans, where he met Jean Lafitte and two other privateers.

The graves exposed by receding waters of Toledo Bend Reservoir, south of present day Pendleton Bridge on *El Camino Real*

When Mary Sharbeno and James Campbell met, she invited him to visit her at Crow's Ferry. Early in 1816 he arrived at the ferry on the Sabine River in a sailing sloop filled with smuggled goods. According to Mary's later memoirs, James Campbell "'soon rendered himself quite the favorite... by virtue of his good humor and the narration...of his haps and mishaps on land and sea.' Following a whirlwind courtship, Mary and James were married in a bond ceremony, and Campbell settled down to a life as a farmer and stockman." [12]

Mary's Sharbeno's family had considerable land holdings, and she had inherited livestock from her father numbering in the hundreds. It was difficult for James to get the sea out of his system, so when Lafitte's recruiter appeared at Crow's Ferry in 1817, Mary's husband convinced her that they belonged on Galveston Island. A few months later the couple arrived at Bolivar Peninsula after traveling overland with a wagon load of their worldly possessions and three hundred farm animals.

James Campbell became Jean Lafitte's most trusted and loyal officer, and served with him until 1821. His reputation was that of a kind man, always treating his captives with mercy; often putting them ashore as soon as possible. Before his death in 1856 at age 70, James Campbell dictated his memoirs to Mirabeau B. Lamar, describing his seafaring adventures in great detail. During her long life, Mary Campbell had nothing but the highest praise for the man who considered her husband his best friend. In her memoirs published in the *Galveston News* in 1884, she described Jean Lafitte as tall, dark, handsome, with black hair, sideburns, and hazel eyes. Mary remembered only one occasion seeing him with a gun. She spoke of him with deepest respect...yes, perhaps he was a privateer, but never, never a pirate! And neither, of course, was her husband!

Mary's mother Margaret Crow continued to operate the ferry on *El Camino Real* with the help of her other children. Her husband Isaac (or Michael) departed one day to attend to business affairs in Mississippi, and never returned. Margaret Crow died in 1826 not knowing what became of him.

In 1819, Crow Ferry was sold to James Gaines, a native of Virginia who came to Texas in 1812 with his cousin, General Edward Pendleton Gaines of the U.S. Army. He owned and operated the ferry with his two sons for the next twenty years. Gaines Ferry, also known as Pendleton Ferry, became the Gateway to Texas no later than 1821. "The main stream of immigrants... both overland and those coming up the Red River by steamboat, merged at

Natchitoches, Louisiana, the last outpost of Anglo-American civilization on the wilderness trek, and followed the King's Highway to Gaines Ferry where they crossed the Sabine River." [13]

On the Texas side of the river the famous Gaines Ferrying House was built, where James provided comfortable lodging for travelers. Stephen F. Austin and his guide Jose Seguin stopped there in 1821 on Austin's first foray into Texas. The soon-to-be most successful Empresario in Mexican Texas met Seguin in Natchitoches, Louisiana. They traveled together down *El Camino Real*, pausing at Fort Jesup before moving westward. On their second night in Texas they enjoyed the hospitality of Gil Y'Barbo's son at *El Lobanillo* before heading further inland on the historic trace through the Ayish Bayou District and Nacogdoches. Stephen F. Austin's first grant contract with the Mexican government was to establish his colony, and bring 300 American settlers into Texas. Austin chose a beautiful, well-watered location near the Brazos and Colorado Rivers, just south of the Camino trace. Austin's Colony was widely publicized with enticing flyers extolling the opportunities for settlement in Texas.

As word spread, the immigrants began arriving, nearly four-fifths of whom chose *El Camino Real* for their entry into Texas. They were met by the large, red-haired, flushed-face man known as James Gaines. The energetic man not only operated the ferry, but collected customs and duties, owned a mercantile business, and was postmaster in the thriving little community of Pendleton he established on the Sabine River. Thomas McFarland surveyed the Pendleton townsite in 1837.

Although the Gaines Ferrying House did not survive its relocation when moved during the building of Toledo Bend Dam and Reservoir, another home built in 1818, The Gaines-Oliphint House, still exists. Cited as the oldest log house in Texas, it was moved to the Pendleton Harbor subdivision where it is being restored by the James Frederick Gomer Chapter, Daughters of the Republic of Texas, Hemphill, Texas.

Black Smoke and Blue Skies: The Paddle-Wheeler Era

The first paddle-wheel steamboat, burning pine knots in its furnace and emitting black smoke from its stack, thump-thump-thumped down the Sabine River in 1837. The *Velocipede* was 120 feet long and 32 feet wide; a shallow draft vessel that drew six feet of water. She traveled all the way to Gaines Ferry to unload the supplies destined for settlements all along *El Camino Real*. The paddle-wheelers were used to haul a variety of cargo, including people and cotton. Early boats on the Sabine River included the *Mady*, the *Ceres*, the *Wisconsin*, the *Sabine* and many others that made regular trips up and down the river. Sadly, most of these old boats sank as a result of striking debris and submerged logs. By 1897 the Riverboat Era had ended. In their final days, the old steam boats transported the supplies used in the construction of the railroads. Ironically, cheaper freight rates by rail were the primary cause of the paddle-wheelers' demise.

*

In 1936 the Texas Highway Department reported that the Gaines (or Pendleton) Ferry was still operating at the old ferry site, having been in continuous use since 1820 and before. The Texas and Louisiana State Highway Departments were still maintaining a day-and-night free ferry service at that time. After the construction of Pendleton Bridge in 1937, ferry service was discontinued on the Sabine River. The rounded-top iron superstructure with steel lacing spanned the river from bank to bank with no underpinnings. It was removed to make way for the current bridge, which stretches over an expanse of nearly two and one-half miles as it crosses Toledo Bend Lake. Construction of this bridge began in late 1965 and was completed in December, 1967.

Three Coins at the Crossing

Because of the myriad of diverse peoples who have traveled the ancient roadway we know as *El Camino Real* many unusual artifacts have been unearthed all along the trail. At the old Sabine River crossing, three Spanish coins minted in Mexico have been found, as follows: An 1804 silver Spanish real coin with all eight pieces intact was found in 2005; in 1996 an 1805 similar coin was found; in August 2005 one-fourth piece of a Spanish real coin was found. Each of these coins had the Spanish King's picture engraved across its face. Other items that have been discovered are a luxury tax token, a coat button from the Civil War, and a yet-to-be-verified button from the war of 1812.

A Grave Mystery

"Sunset and evening star, and one clear call for me!
And may there be no moaning of the bar, when I put out to sea....
Twilight and evening bell, and after that, the dark!
And may there be no sadness of farewell, when I embark;
For though from out our bourne of Time and Place the flood may bear me far,
I hope to see my Pilot face to face when I have crossed the bar."

—Alfred Lord Tennyson

Weldon McDaniel, Sabine County's Historical Commission Chairman, is one of the most knowledgeable historians to be found anywhere. We met him on the Texas side of the Pendleton Bridge at the beautiful new pavilion built by Texas Garden Clubs, Inc. and the Hemphill Garden Club. On this hot July day Weldon had brought the three coins for us to see, and he wanted to show us "the graves." The water level of Toledo Bend Reservoir had gone down more than six feet in the summer drought. As the lake receded, a long forgotten cemetery became exposed. Being the meticulous historian that he is, Commission Chairman McDaniel has measured all seventy-one discernable graves and platted their locations in grid fashion. The neatly arranged rows contain graves of varied sizes...both single and double. Sadly, there are forty-four smaller, child-size graves, indicating the rigors of travel and disease on these young travelers. With the exception of one, all the graves are in an east-west configuration, denoting Christian burial style. None of the graves have monuments. McDaniel's conjecture is that these burials were of Texas' earliest immigrants. Perhaps a goodly portion of these settlers died in transit from Georgia, Alabama, Tennessee and other states. Not wishing to bury their deceased along the trail, the families covered the bodies with lime, wrapped them in sheets, and continued in their wagons until reaching the Texas side of the Sabine River, "the promised land." Crossing the ferry, the family took advantage of the first land available for burial.

A roll of thunder brought an end to our nostalgia. Ominous storm clouds rolled in, and the lake's placid surface was suddenly transformed into a sea of angry, white capping waves. As gale force winds began to blow, we rushed to the safety of our automobile. Later, thinking about fate and circumstance, we were reminded of how the settlers arriving in primitive conditions were at the mercy of the unpredictable, ever-changing weather.

Several days later we traveled by boat from East Hamilton to the "watery gravesite" to take close-up pictures. It was a sad, surreal experience. Once again we realized the magnitude of the tragedies that had befallen these early people. What a price these forebears paid in their quest to dwell in this fertile land called Texas! We often take their sacrifices for granted.

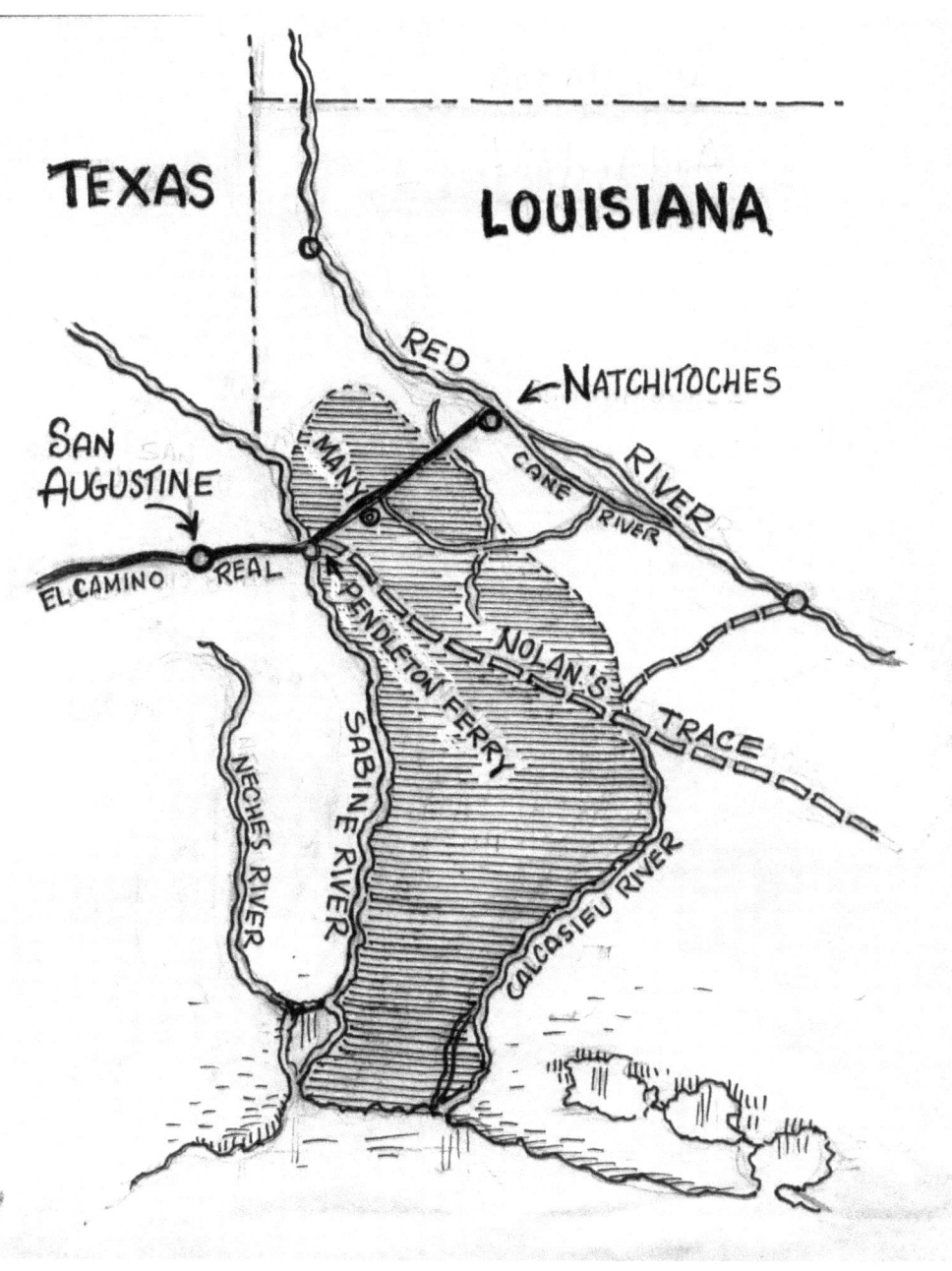

A close approximation of No Man's Land Boundaries
Sketch by Richard Murphy

Chapter Five

No Place To Be:

<u>No Man's Land: The Neutral Strip</u>

The wind was a torrent of darkness among the gusty trees,
The moon was a ghostly galleon tossed upon cloudy seas,
The road was a ribbon of moonlight over the purple moor,
and the highwayman came riding, riding, riding...
The highwayman came riding, up to the old inn door.
                    Alfred Noyes

Oftentimes the destiny of inhabitants in a given locale is determined by the flourish of a pen; the signatures of political or military leaders as lands are bought, claimed or divided. Such was the case with the creation of The Neutral Strip in 1806. The area was entered with trepidation by decent, law-abiding folk, most of whom needed several days to cross the forty-mile wide territory. Alfred Noyes' poem quoted above expresses the eerie sense of foreboding felt by the travelers as their wagons creaked and groaned over the deep ruts of *El Camino Real*. Even the silence was stifling.

Spain had returned Louisiana to France in 1802. By May 1803, Robert Livingston and James Monroe signed a purchase treaty with France making Louisiana a part of the United States. U.S. Army General James Wilkinson ordered the establishment of Fort Claiborne in 1805 at Natchitoches, with a sizeable contingent of troops headquartered there. Spain was not pleased with this turn of events, sending Captain Joseph Gonzales and several patrols of soldiers from Nacogdoches across the Sabine River in an effort to reclaim all the *Los Adaes* area to the Rio Hondo. He was met by Captain Edward D. Turner and soldiers from Fort Claiborne. Of course, both "Spanish and United States officers were aware of the claims of their respective countries... both willing to fight...but having the intelligence and initiative to declare a stalemate to prevent a war." On February 6, 1806 Captain Gonzales signed the document agreeing to "return all troops of his Catholic Majesty's to the other side of the Rio Sabinas."[14]

This agreement established the Neutral Strip, or the Free State of Sabine, a forty-mile wide area between the Sabine and the Rio Hondo. It included Nolan's Trace, the trail blazed by Philip Nolan in 1801 for transporting horses from Texas. Unfortunately, *El Camino Real*, the busiest and most important artery for transportation of people and goods, went right through it. Without policing from either the United States or Spain, the "strip became one of the most lawless places that ever existed within the confines of the United States...every outlaw and murderer made this Neutral Strip his destination... the only safe way to cross the strip was to travel in force, therefore, either at Natchitoches or on the west side of Sabine River, the travelers waited until a large enough group was gathered to guarantee safe travel. The outlaws dealt in horse stealing, cattle rustling, counterfeiting, or any other form of crime that might strike their fancy."[15]

Historian and artist Richard Murphy tells the story of one of the most ruthless outlaw families living in the Neutral Strip in 1820. We quote:

> "Just across the Sabine in No Man's Land lived old Jesse Yocum and his sons. The Yocums were typical of the dangerous people who infested this area. The notorious clan had been run out of Kentucky and later Natchez, Mississippi, and like other men with unsavory pasts, they settled in the Neutral Ground. From this haven the family engaged in...illegal activities, preying with impunity on people on both sides of the river." After one of the Yocum's murdering and kidnaping episodes they were finally run out of the area by young settler David Renfroe and his neighbors. Murphy's story continues: "Their trips into Texas had proven mighty unhealthy for the Yocums, but the family kept pushing their luck. ...Under the leadership of Thomas Yocum they settled on Pine Island Bayou, where Thomas built a combination inn and saloon. Almost immediately he and his family began to rob and kill travelers. Traveling men could be traced to Yocum's Inn and were never heard from again. After a score of such disappearances the citizens decided to investigate. A posse was formed which scoured the woods around Yocum's place. Several bodies were found and one skeleton in an old well...Thomas Yocum managed to...escape into the deep woods, but his pursuers, with the help of bloodhounds, were able to track him down and, somewhere in the Big Thicket, they captured and hanged him to a tree."

"No Place To Be" lasted fifteen years, from 1806 to 1821.

"The proclamation of the Adams-Onis Treaty of Washington in 1821 fixed the western boundary of the United States as the Sabine River, thus the agreement with the Mexican Republic transferred the Neutral Strip to the United States...ownership backed by the Army soon restored peace and order to No Man's Land" [16]

Fort Jesup near Many, Louisiana

Fort Jesup

In March of 1822 Lieutenant Colonel Zachary Taylor received a letter from General Edmund P. Gaines instructing him to establish a position on "the southwestern frontier of Louisiana to defend and protect its inhabitants." Taylor selected a site on a hill between the watersheds of the Red River and the Sabine River for a permanent command post adjacent to *El Camino Real*. The new cantonment was named Fort Jesup.

"Colonel James B. Many, the fort's commandant, was there to greet Stephen Fuller Austin and his emigrants on their way into Texas in 1823. Such important men as David Crockett, James Bowie, Stephen F. Austin and Sam Houston; and such famous scouts as Ben S. Lilly and 'Big Foot' Wallace visited there. Because they were welcomed and entertained at Fort Jesup, accusations were made by the Spanish that it was a meeting place for those planning the overthrow of the Mexican government. And this may very well have been true, for supplies necessary for the conduct of the war for Texas independence undoubtedly passed through Fort Jesup." [17]

Historic Old North Church, Nacogdoches, Texas

Chapter Six

Give Me That Old Time Religion...
Early Missionaries and Historic Churches Along Camino Real

"For the Lord your God is bringing you into a good land, a land of brooks of water,
of fountains and springs, flowing forth in valleys and hills...
a land in which you will eat bread without scarcity,
in which you will lack nothing...And you shall eat and be full,
and you shall bless the Lord your God for the good land He has given you."
Deuteronomy 8: 7, 9, 10

All along *El Camino Real* in East Texas...through its cities, towns and countryside...the present-day traveler sees churches of every denomination dotting the landscape, sentinels of the heritage established by our forebears in generations past. The pioneer Texans of the 1820's had many concerns relating to survival: claiming title to their lands, protecting their families from Indians and the outlaw element, planting and harvesting, and building secure dwellings. Their faith in God sustained them through many trials and hardships as they carved out new lives in primitive Texas. Having come to Texas from mostly civilized locales, the settlers' next priority centered on building churches and schools. Many of these institutions used the same building; often the early schools were closely affiliated with church denominations.

Although the Mexican Colonization Law excluded all religions except Roman Catholic, the settlers who came from Protestant backgrounds mostly worshiped as they pleased in private homes and camp meetings as early as 1819-1820. They enjoyed the lively, evangelistic sermons of preachers like Baptists Joseph Bays, William Biddle, and Z.N. Morrell; Methodists William and James P. Stevenson, Needham J. Alford and Francis Wilson; Cumberland Presbyterian Sumner Bacon; and Church of Christ minister Dr. William Defee.

The Mexican authorities were not overly concerned about the spiritual pursuits of the settlers, as long as they didn't cause trouble. When ferry-keeper James Gaines complained to Colonel Jose Piedras, the commandant at

Nacogdoches, about the two-day camp meeting held by Alford and Bacon in 1832 near present-day Milam he asked, "'Are they stealing any horses? Are they killing anybody? Are they doing anything bad?' Receiving a negative reply to each question, Piedras added, 'Let them alone.'" [18]

In 1833 Reverend James P. Stevenson held two "class meetings" at the home of Samuel Doak McMahan, which led to the formation of a Methodist Society. After freedom from Mexico, the first log McMahan Chapel was built in 1837 under the leadership of Reverend Littleton Fowler, one of the first missionaries to Texas. Today, historical markers designate it as the first Protestant and Methodist Church in Texas with continuous services. The current McMahan Chapel was constructed in 1949, and contains some of the most magnificent stained glass windows anywhere. The tombstone of Littleton Fowler has been incorporated into the altar area of the Church. McMahan Chapel and Conference Center is located ten miles east of San Augustine, just off Highway 21. According to church treasurer and historian Bobbie Lou Thompson, one of the original branches of *El Camino Real* veered southward at El Lobanillo Creek and meandered its way to the present McMahan Chapel and adjoining historic cemetery. Just down the hill from the Chapel early worshipers met around a still freely flowing spring that has come to be known as "The Wellspring of Protestantism."

Cumberland Presbyterian Sumner Bacon, commissioned by the American Bible Society, "had distributed thousands of Bibles in both English and Spanish by 1832. He reported in 1834 that in the civil jurisdiction of Nacogdoches, extending from the Trinity River to the Sabine, there were about 600 American families and 300 Spanish families, and that the households destitute of the Bible were about nine to one. He called for at least 500 Bibles for immediate distribution in the East Texas area, and organized the first Bible Society in Texas." [19]

An eloquent letter written by hero of the Alamo William Barrett Travis to the New York Christian Advocate on August 17, 1835 provides an interesting glimpse into his thoughts:

> "My Dear Sir: I take the liberty of addressing you from this distant quarter of the world for the purpose of requesting you to receive my name as a subscriber of your widely circulated Christian

Advocate...Although the exercise of religion is not prohibited here, but is encouraged by the people, yet but few preachers have come among us to dispense the tidings of salvation to upwards of sixty thousand souls... About five educated and talented young preachers would find employment in Texas, and no doubt would produce much good in this benighted land. Texas is composed of the shrewdest and most intelligent population of any new country on earth, therefore, a preacher to do good must be respectable and talented. In sending your heralds to the four corners of the earth, remember Texas. William B. Travis"

By 1837 missionaries Martin Ruter and Robert Alexander were in Texas at the Gaines Ferrying House, where they spent the entire night making plans for evangelizing the foreign mission field of Texas.

With the coming of Texas Independence and open religious freedom, churches of many denominations began to spring up all over East Texas. In 1837, "The Pilgrim Church, a Primitive or "Hardshell" Baptist of the "Two Seed" variety, under the guidance of Daniel Parker was directly responsible for the first Baptist church to be organized in Texas, Hopewell Baptist Church near Douglass."[20] Parker also founded the oldest Baptist church in Sabine County, Bethel Church, (now New Hope Church) near Milam in 1841.

San Augustine claims several "first" churches in Texas: First Methodist, 1837; Memorial Presbyterian, 1838; Antioch Church of Christ, 1833; and Jerusalem C.M.E., 1845. Mrs. James Pinckney Henderson, wife of Texas' first governor, was the driving force in organizing Christ Episcopal Church in both San Augustine and Nacogdoches in 1848. St. Augustine Catholic Church traces its roots back to the early mission days, 1717.

Melrose has two churches with historical significance: Melrose Baptist, founded in 1854, and Melrose Methodist, established in 1860. Tindall wrote, "The first Missionary Baptist Church organized in Nacogdoches was the Union Baptist Church, known today as the Old North Church, in May, 1838...Elder Isaac Reed and church clerk C.H. Whitaker were instrumental in the early success of the church. Union Baptist Church met for several years in the Liberty School House, a red-oak log building...first of a number of school houses which served the citizens as schools and religious meeting places."[21]

First cornerstone of a Methodist church in San Augustine, Texas
Built in 1838 by MasterArchitect Augustus Phelps

San Augustine Methodist Church built 1907

Christ Episcopal Church, San Augustine, Texas

"Littleton Fowler arrived in Nacogdoches on October 16, 1837, accompanied by John B. Denton, a local preacher whom Fowler had employed before leaving Arkansas. By January 1838 Fowler had acquired deeds to lots in Nacogdoches, San Augustine, Washington-on-the-Brazos, and Houston. Not only had he acquired the lots, but he also had acquired adequate subscriptions for building (Methodist) churches on the lots." [22]

"The history of the Catholic Church in Nacogdoches...began when the Franciscans established Nuestra Senora de Guadalupe and continues today as the Sacred Heart Church. To read its history is to read the history of Nacogdoches.... The Parish was founded in 1847 by Rev. John M. Odin... Father C.M. Chambodut served as the first pastor." [23]

Old Palestine Church on *El Camino Real* three miles east of Alto is one of the oldest Protestant churches in East Texas. The present church was built in 1848. Many pioneer families are buried in the historic cemetery nearby.

According to author Clyde McQueen, "The Zion Hill First Baptist Church in Nacogdoches was organized in 1879. The historic church is an imposing Gothic Revival and Victorian edifice built in 1914 by German-born architect Dietrich Antone Wilhelm Rulfs. Although the congregation no longer meets there, efforts are currently underway by preservationists to restore the structure." [24]

Near Geneva, Texas is the County Line Missionary Baptist Church, founded soon after the Civil War in 1868 in the freedmen's community known as Weeks Quarters. The church was organized under the leadership of Rev. Alfredo Canton. County Line Church is still extremely active, serving members from both Sabine and San Augustine Counties. [25]

Also near Geneva is the New Zion United Methodist Church, established in 1891. Adjacent to the church is the William Gasby Cemetery, named for a prominent leader in the black community who was instrumental in developing the town of Geneva. The cemetery is located on four acres of land donated by Gasby in 1870, to be used by the neighboring black community. [26]

According to author Pearl Travis, "Churches grew up in the vicinity of Chireno. One of the early churches of Methodists was near where the lower cemetery is. A union church a few miles out near the Little Community served Methodists, Baptists, and others for many years. This church, called Old Friendship, was finally the parent Baptist Church of Chireno organized in 1878." [27] The city of Crockett is home to some of East Texas' earliest churches. The Methodist Church was founded in 1839 with Rev. Henderson Palmer as organizing pastor, and First Baptist of Crockett followed soon afterward in 1846. The Bethel Baptist Church was organized in 1869. Every year on December 31st the citizens of Crockett look forward to the tolling of the Church bell as it rings in the new year. Several other churches in Crockett with interesting histories are more than 100 years old: Saint Paul Baptist Church established in 1885; St. Luke's Baptist Church founded in 1902; and St. Andrew A.M.E. Church established in 1903. First Christian Church was founded in 1901, with Rev. Harry Hamilton as the first pastor. Before the church was built their services were held in the Houston County Courtroom.

Every time we are in Crockett a drive by the beautiful Mary Allen Academy building is a "must." For years we've commented that this magnificent old landmark, constructed in 1886, deserves to be saved and restored. Although this isn't a church as such, it was originally established as a college for black females by the Northern Presbyterian Church. The students were required to be high school graduates, and most were seventeen and eighteen years old. In later years the denomination changed to a Baptist college, and became co-educational, with male students admitted as well as females. At last it seems that restoration has become a possibility. According to Agnes Rhoder, committee chairperson for the project, the building has been purchased, and plans are moving along now to establish the *Mary Allen Museum of African American History and Art* in this visible location close to downtown Crockett.

The Weeping Mary Baptist Church, located just north of *El Camino Real* and about 6.5 miles west of Alto, is called "Best Church Name" by Bob Bowman in *The Best of East Texas*. The little village of less than forty residents began after the Civil War when freed slaves moved to the area and named the settlement and church for Mary Magdalene, who wept at the tomb of Jesus, as recorded in the Gospel of John, Chapter 20. The Weeping Mary Baptist Church, now more than 120 years old, was used in years past as "a community school that served black children in the Neches River bottomlands." [28]

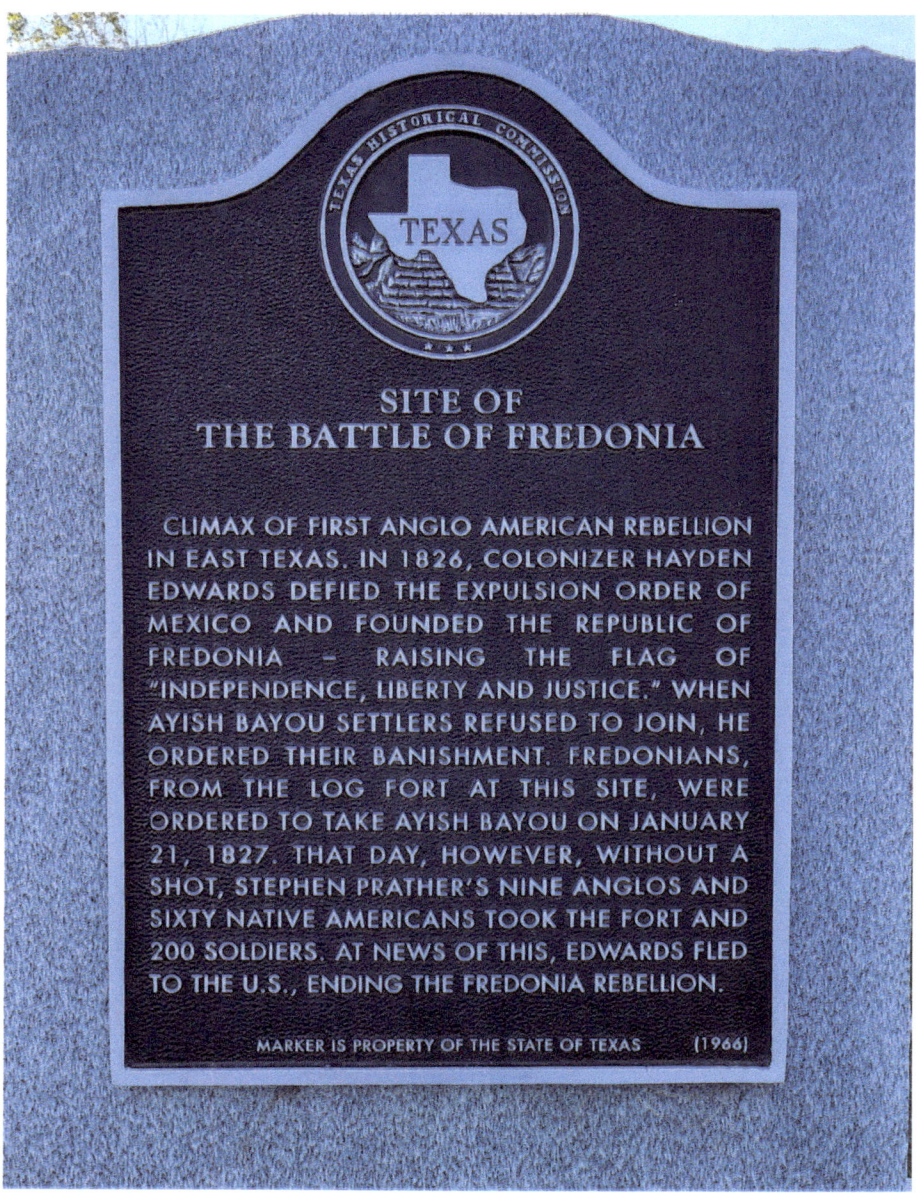

Historic Landmark (RTHL) located 2 miles from downtown San Augustine, just east of the Deep East Texas Electric Cooperative on Texas Highway 21 East

Chapter Seven

The Fredonian Rebellion: A Search for the Decisive Battleground

The story of the Edwards brothers and the events surrounding the Fredonian Rebellion are of such widespread significance and far-reaching consequences throughout East Texas and along *El Camino Real* as to require a separate chapter for this subject. Such noted authors as Dr. Archie McDonald in *Texas: All Hail the Mighty State*, Dr. George L. Crocket in *Two Centuries in East Texas*, Hodding Carter in *Doomed Road of Empire*, and Jack Jackson in *Indian Agent: Peter Ellis Bean in Mexican Texas* provide detailed, well-documented accounts of this tumultuous period. The *Diary of Alexander Horton* gives a first-hand description of the closing events from a young participant's perspective. For the sake of brevity a summarized version follows:

Americans entering Texas in the mid-1820's liked the Mexican Constitution of 1824 for the freedom it provided them in settling the land according to Mexico's national colonization law. Becoming peaceful Mexican citizens did not seem bothersome, nor did the requirement to claim Catholicism as their religion. "They came for inexpensive or free land, and such requirements were well worth the price of an oath." [29]

On April 15, 1825 "Haden Edwards received an empresarial grant to the lands around Nacogdoches and extending down the Trinity, Neches, Angelina and Sabine Rivers." [30]

Unlike the undeveloped area selected by Empresario Stephen F. Austin for his Colony, Edwards' grant encompassed the ancient heartland of Texas, a well-populated and long-established territory. Its gateway was *El Camino Real*, the King's Highway, through which the majority of immigrants had come. Most of the lands had been settled and claimed for many years; whether or not the owners possessed valid titles, or titles at all, became the problem at hand. Dr. Crocket describes Edwards as "an amiable and accomplished gentleman and a man of honor...his chief difficulty seems to have been a lack of practical wisdom in dealing with men, a failure to adapt himself to the conditions which surrounded him, conditions which demanded this quality more than any other." [31]

Certainly these traits were unlike Stephen F. Austin, who was a master of diplomacy and patience in dealing with both the Mexican officials and his colonists. Austin did his best to convince Edwards to exercise caution.

"Edwards posted a notice at the Stone Fort in Nacogdoches to inform all prior claimants that they would have to come to him and prove ownership of all lands within his grant, or they would be assumed to be his and could be sold to new settlers." [32]

Official titles issued to Ayish Bayou District residents Elisha Roberts, Edmund Quirk, Richard Sims, and James Quinalty were among only a few with legal documentation of their claims. Understandably, the settlers were displeased with this turn of events, and complained to the Mexican government. At the end of October 1826 Haden Edwards received his eviction notice. His contract was annulled and he was expelled from Texas.

"Instead, Haden's brother, Benjamin Edwards declared their grant area as the free state of Fredonia...(and) some of the Cherokees under the leadership of John Hunter and Richard Fields joined the Edwards brothers in the Fredonia movement. On December 16, 1826 the Fredonia Republic flew its red and white flag symbolizing the Anglo and Indian Alliance. It proclaimed *Independence, Liberty and Justice* in bold letters along with signatures of several of the supporters of this pretender government." [33]

This turn of events was viewed with consternation by both Mexican officials and Empresario Stephen F. Austin. Eloquent, rational pleas were sent to the Edwards brothers and Indian leaders Fields and Hunter to cease and desist, but to no avail. Austin's substantial militia and a contingent of Mexican troops headed toward East Texas.

Before their arrival, Haden Edwards sent a company of 100 men into the Ayish Bayou District, giving the people there fifteen days to comply with his edict. Elisha Roberts wrote: "It appears at present impossible to say which side to take to save our families and property. ...the only course to pursue is to lie still and take no part on any side. The people of this vicinity intended to try to put down the rebellion, until they were informed that the Indians had joined them."

During the mass exodus that followed, most of the people fled across the Sabine, and there were only two families left...Alexander Horton and his mother, and a quite elderly Edward Teal. Horton was only seventeen at the time. Later in life, he recounted the events that followed:

"Our prospects were gloomy indeed, and from the Attoyac to the Sabine...all had fled to save their property...all hope seemed to be gone when the comforter came. There was a noble old soldier by the name of Stephen Prather...who at that time was keeping an Indian Store on the Angelina...On learning of our distressed situation he at once raised all the forces he could and came to our assistance. Prather had raised about sixty or seventy Indians, all armed and painted for war...my old friend Prather rode up and took me by the hand, and said, 'Not run away yet?' I said to him: 'No, that I was still there.'.... He asked if I did not want to go with him and assist in taking the Fredonian fort. I answered that I would, for I was glad of an opportunity to assist in saving my country from being broken up. I at once saddled my horse and took my faithful old rifle and fell into line.

"It was a motley crowd, but it was the only chance, for our hopes were gone. We had but few white men. I well remember them all and will give their names. There were Col. Prather and his two sons, Stephen and Freeman; Ross Bridges, James Bridges Sr. and James Bridges Jr., Peter Galloway, John McGinnis and A. Horton. These, with the Indians, were all that we had to meet the Fredonians, who were well fortified, having two double log houses and other outhouses. An Indian is an ugly sight when painted and dressed for war...At daylight Prather formed his men in regular form of battle and marched upon their fort. When in about fifty yards of the fort he gave the order to charge...the Indians raised the warwhoop at the same time, which is a most dreadful yell. This completely unnerved the Fredonians. Without firing a gun, the thing was settled, as Col. Prather ordered his men not to fire a gun or kill any man unless fired upon by them.

"The next thing was to arrest the other Fredonians who were coming down from Nacogdoches to reinforce them, for that was the day that they were to be down to carry out their decree of confiscation... Our men formed in regular order on the roadside...about ten o'clock they began to come in squads of ten or twelve in number, and as fast as they arrived were taken and disarmed." [34]

There is no doubt that the Mexican forces would have quickly and easily defeated the Fredonians, who could not seem to muster the general support from the populace they desired.. And it is fortunate that the entire six-week episode was ended without bloodshed. A lengthy list of men who supported Mexico in both thought and action included such well-known persons as Peter Ellis Bean, James Gaines, and, as mentioned, Stephen F. Austin, whose primary concern was the continued success of his colony. The Fredonians were well represented by not only Haden and Benjamin Edwards, but by Adolphus Sterne and Martin Parmer. And yet, differences and animosity were forgotten a few years later when men such as Austin, Parmer, Sterne and Gaines joined hands in the successful struggle for Texas Independence.

*

John Sprowl of the Ayish Bayou District was one of the sympathizers on the side of the Fredonians. His home place, and the site of the closing battle of the Fredonian Rebellion, is located on *El Camino Real*, Highway 21, approximately two miles east of San Augustine. The John Sprowl place is now owned by Dr. C.R. and Mary Jean Haley, who live nearby in an impressive plantation-style home that sits atop a hill overlooking the Royal Road. In the 1800's *El Camino Real* was an old wagon trace that traversed the Haley property just south of the present road, then meandered behind the modern Deep East Texas Electric Cooperative area headquarters. An invitation from the doctor resulted in a several-hour trek through his land in search of the elusive John Sprowl spring and Fredonian campground. It has been our experience that interviews and on-site visits to historic locations elicit information more authentically exciting and valid...somehow "being there" stokes the fires of the imagination. As we began to walk, Dr. Haley mentioned the inaccessibility of the location; we would have to probe our way through dense undergrowth to reach the site as he remembered it. Upon our arrival we found the Sprowl spring and surrounding area completely overgrown with privet hedge, bramble-briars and wild roses. We reached the stream's bank, wondering if the spring that had slaked the thirst of many weary travelers was dry, or still flowing. We found the old spring still there, with sunlight filtering through towering trees and refracting off its surface. Cool, clear, refreshing water bubbled forth, a rewarding sight. For those early pioneers nearly two hundred years ago who came this way, it would have been a welcome life saver.

John Spowl Spring, still flowing, just east of San Augustine, Texas

Stephen F. Austin commerative marker located in front of the Old Stone Fort,
campus of SFASU, Nacogdoches, Texas
Erected by the Sons of the Republic of Texas

Chapter Eight

By the Way: A Journey Westward on El Camino Real

"Let me live in a house by the side of the road, where the race of men go by,
the men who are good and the men who are bad, as good and as bad as I.
I see from my house by the side of the road, by the side of the highway of life,
The men who press with the ardor of hope, the men who are faint with the strife.
But I turn not away from their smiles nor their tears, both part of an infinite plan,
Let me live in a house by the side of the road, and be a friend to man."
Sam Walter Foss

El Camino Real is a road of friendship and common heritage for East Texans who call the lands between the Sabine and Trinity Rivers home. During its lifetime of more than three centuries Our Road has come full-circle...from foot travel, horses and covered wagons in the beginning to the most modern of vehicular traffic today. There are wayside rest areas and convenient stops along the way for the travelers in thousands of cars and trucks who speed down the famous, well-paved highway each day. *El Camino Real* is unique among Texas highways: our journey takes us by the familiar pink granite markers, past frequent brown historical road signs, numerous Recorded Texas Historic Landmarks and Centennial monuments... all serving to remind us that Our Road is special, different from all the others throughout the State in sheer quantity of historic designations. The towns and cities somehow seem innately connected, too, as each is dissected by the historic trail.

Milam

In 1828 Milam was known as Red Mound. This was a descriptive name for the settlement, since ridges to the east were rich in iron ore, causing the soil to be a rich, burnt-red color. By 1835 the name had been changed to Milam, in honor of Texas hero Benjamin Rush Milam, who died in the Battle of Bexar during the early stages of the struggle for Texas Independence. We interviewed a longtime Milam resident, a very historically knowledgeable Billy Fussell, on a number of occasions. Milam was the home of John C. Hale, one of the few Texans killed in the Battle of San Jacinto. The little village was incorporated in 1837. Because of its strategic location just across the Sabine River, it was an International Revenue Post where customs and duties were collected during the Republic of Texas days. Masonry continues to be important today, much as it was in the early days; Milam's first Lodge was founded in 1840; today it is Sexton Lodge #251. From 1861-1865 the town was headquarters for the Quartermaster's Department of the Confederacy. Sabine County's first seat of government was in Milam until 1858, when it was moved to the more centrally located Hemphill. The present-day post office occupies the former location of the County Courthouse.

Fussell's photograph of Milam during the early 1900's showed a rather successful town. The old courthouse was still visible; the business district showed a Woodmen of the World building, a blacksmith shop, and Gilbert McKechney's store, where Sam Houston once bought two shirts. Nethery's Antiques, founded in 1880, is still in business. The fire department and library continue to be assets to the community.

A big event each year is Milam Settlers Day, always held the weekend before Thanksgiving, rain or shine. People comes from miles around to El Camino Park at the intersection of Highways 21 and 87 to enjoy crafts, music, food and the Little Miss Milam Day Pageant, all under the direction of event coordinator Jeannie Thomas.

Las Borregas Creek and Campsite

Located on State Highway 21 just west of Milam is Las Borregas Creek. Upstream a short distance from the campsite the Spanish had an army post to protect travelers around 1800. This site is of special interest because Stephen F. Austin spent his first night in Texas on July 16, 1821, on Las Borregas Creek.

Geneva

A very prominently located Texas Historical Marker alongside *El Camino Real* in Geneva, Texas is the site of Gil Y'Barbo's Ranch, *El Lobanillo*, already mentioned in a previous chapter. Geneva still has an aura of historic ambiance about it, although its reputation as a prosperous agricultural community in the early 1900's is long gone. The town was first called Jimtown, for two of the early settlers, Jim Halbert and Jim Willis. "It is considered the oldest continuously occupied site in East Texas having roots dating back to September, 1794 when Spain granted to Juan Ignatio Pifermo four leagues of land lying in the vicinity of the present-day community." [35]

Until 1920 Geneva had five retail stores, a cotton gin, gristmill, hotel, sawmill and livery stable. Early store owners included D.S. Dean, T.E. Alford, C.A. and B.D. Jones. Later, Charlie Minton, Roy Harris, Shorty Graham and Elzie (Bill) Low were storekeepers. Bill's wife Gertrude was the postmistress in Geneva for many years. Dr. Robert Chapman was one of the best known early doctors in Sabine County. He attended the sick day and night, often riding horseback into the wee hours, tying himself in the saddle in the event he fell asleep.

El Lobanillo Marker, Geneva, Texas

The New Orleans Greys

In New Orleans, on October 11, 1835, a large, enthusiastic crowd gathered for the meeting being held on behalf of Texas. There were placards everywhere calling for volunteers, and the newspapers proclaimed support for the Americans in Texas against the tyranny of Mexico's president, Santa Anna. A young, adventuresome German boy named Herman Ehrenberg was one of the sixty-five volunteers who made up the first company of the New Orleans Greys; the men who would enter Texas by way of *El Camino Real* and make their way to San Antonio. A second company would go by ship to the Texas coast. Adolphus Sterne from Nacogdoches was in New Orleans as the Texas recruiter. Before leaving New Orleans the next day each volunteer was outfitted in a grey uniform suitable for prairie life, and a rifle, pistol and Bowie knife. Upon reaching the Sabine the Greys kissed the soil of their new land, and accepted a beautiful blue silk flag, handmade by East Texas ladies and inscribed in honor of the New Orleans Greys...a flag flown over the Alamo only a few months later. Although no one is certain, many believe the Greys' flag was made by ladies in San Augustine, whose flag-making abilities are well documented. Henson and Parmelee relate such incidents in their Cartwright book, mentioning that a banner for "The San Augustine Volunteers" of William Kimbro's Company in March 1836 was made by "Misses Amanda and America Holman, Mrs. Augustus Hotchkiss, and Mrs. Parks." During the Civil War, Anna and Mary Cartwright presented a flag to Captain Benjamin Franklin Benton's men upon their departure in 1861. [36]

As the eager recruits traveled down *El Camino Real* they were greeted all along the way with the hospitality for which East Texans are still famous. At San Augustine, the Greys enjoyed tables heaped with beefsteaks and wild game; warm, crackling fires in the homes of colonists; covers for their beds of bear and buffalo skins.

Ehrenberg described forests and prairies as the Greys traveled along *El Camino Real* into Nacogdoches. It was late, and the men were exhausted. They knocked at the door of a large, two-story house that was none other than the home of Squire Sterne, who was expecting them. (In addition to the recruits, Adolphus Sterne had raised $10,000 in New Orleans for the Texas cause.) Before leaving Nacogdoches the Greys were given a celebration banquet shared by both colonists and volunteers. Ehrenberg related the events of the farewell evening:

Sterne-Hoya Home, Nacogdoches, Texas

"In the midst of our table there stood a large black bear, nicknamed Mr. Petz. This huge creature, which was the main dish of our menu, was so skillfully dressed in his fur that he seemed to be alive; his mouth drawn back in a fierce grin and showed sharp, white teeth tightly holding the true colors of the 1824 Constitution. Raccoons, opossums, squirrels and turkeys surrounded Mr. Petz, while two large legs of mutton roasted to a nice brown, and a substantial joint of beef completed the decoration of our board." [37]

Before leaving Nacogdoches the Greys obtained horses for the rest of their journey to San Antonio. By November they were with the Texans near San Antonio under the command of General Edward Burleson. Ehrenberg was with Ben Milam during the siege on San Antonio. He was involved in the Matamoros expedition, and was with James Fannin at Coleto. He miraculously escaped the massacre at Goliad. Ehrenberg's story of his experiences in Texas were first published in 1843 in German, after he returned home. It was a popular book, believed to be instrumental in attracting German settlers to Texas in the 1840's and 1850's.

San Augustine

El Camino Real from Geneva to San Augustine is still a winding roadway amidst dense forests and stream-fed hillsides. It is really quite easy to imagine the trail before 1936 and 1937, when the eastern section of Highway 21 was paved. Ten miles east of San Augustine the traveler passes the McMahan Chapel roadside monument and the directional marker to the Chapel and Conference Center. Soon after, Ford's Corner and the access road to the historic Abney-Scurlock Cemetery appears. Within a few miles the entrance to Fairway Farm, a famous golf and hunt club during the mid-20th century, appears on the south side of the historic trail.

Closer to San Augustine on the north side of *El Camino Real* is a Centennial monument denoting the location of Elisha Roberts home: a haven of hospitality to travelers for several decades. We are indebted to his descendant, Martha Gill Roberts Pay, for providing us with information from her extensive Roberts family history.

Elisha and Martha Gill Roberts came to the Ayish Bayou District in 1823, one of the earliest American pioneer families entering the area. Elisha had served in the War of 1812; his father before him had served with General George Washington at Valley Forge in 1778. The Roberts family settled near the "old brick springs" about five miles east of Ayish Bayou. Elisha erected one of the first cotton gins in the district, and by 1831 had been elected Alcalde of the territory. Stories are told of Elisha "holding court" on the porch of his home, and welcoming frequent visitors like Sam Houston. A seasoned, common-sense leader, he was one of the committee of fifteen men selected in 1832 to choose the site for the town of San Augustine. The chosen locale was on the east bank of Ayish Bayou, near the site of *Dolores Mission*. Surveyor Thomas McFarland laid out the town in 1833, the first in Texas designed according to the American plan, i.e., a courthouse square surrounded by streets and blocks. Elisha was also one of the original trustees of the University of San Augustine.

Nowadays the small community of San Augustine is considered, for the most part, a peaceful, neighborly, law-abiding town. Martha Pay relates a story concerning her grandfather, Sheriff Noel Gill Roberts III, indicating this was not always the case. In 1900 a feud on the Courthouse square nearly brought an end to the new sheriff's career. His brother and uncle were killed in the skirmish, and Noel was seriously wounded by two bullets. Dr. Felix Tucker, a relative, and Rev. George L. Crocket, rector of Christ Episcopal Church, were able to enter the courthouse and help Noel to his horse while dodging bullets. "Next morning Sheriff Roberts was taken over to Nacogdoches, leaving behind a town almost beside itself with dread and apprehension. Desperate appeals went to the Governor, and he ordered the Stone Fort Rifles from Nacogdoches to get to San Augustine as fast as they could....by June 6, 1900 the Rifles had enforced the Governor's decree of martial law, and order was restored." [38]

Matthew Cartwright home built in 1839 by Augustus Phelps, San Augustine, Texas

Elisha Roberts' son-in-law was Philip Sublett, whose home was a short distance from the Roberts property. Sublett family members still live on the original homesite, although their current home, built in 1874, replaced the earlier home that burned. It was Phil Sublett who nominated his friend Sam Houston as Commander in Chief of the Texan Forces, a nomination ratified later in Nacogdoches. After the victory at San Jacinto, Houston recuperated from his serious ankle wound at the Sublett home, welcomed by his many friends in San Augustine.

Artist Penelope Thomas, the eighteen-year-old daughter of Houston's close friend I. D. Thomas, asked General Sam Houston to sit for a portrait in 1858 during one of his frequent visits to San Augustine. Houston was sixty-three years old at the time. Descendants of the Thomas family still own this rare and uncirculated portrait of the Texas hero. Penelope, the aunt of renowned artist S. Seymour Thomas, was the first to discover the artistic abilities of the young boy. She became his first art teacher, encouraging him in the development of his talent. Seymour Thomas' portrait of "General Sam Houston on Horseback" during the Battle of San Jacinto hangs prominently in the museum of the San Jacinto Monument, and is one of his most famous works.

Members of the Price family tell the legendary story of their ancestor, Cornelia Price, the beautiful Belle of San Augustine in 1840, when San Augustine's society and culture were at a peak. The eldest daughter of planter-merchant Colonel Elijah Price and his wife Temperance, Cornelia was taught music, art, needlework, and dancing, as were her five sisters. Her five brothers were educated to become doctors, lawyers, and fine gentlemen. The Price home faced *El Camino Real* just east of San Augustine. It was a spacious, Southern style house with plenty of room for the large family and the enjoyment of many friends.

The eighteen-year-old Cornelia did not lack for suitors. Many young men were captivated by her blue eyes, lustrous black hair, and graceful manner. Charles Rush Sossaman, the silversmith's son, was deeply in love with Cornelia, and longed to make her his wife. Nevertheless, her admirers were all forgotten with the arrival of a charming and chivalrous young Frenchman from New Orleans, LeBleu Fontaine, who opened a dancing school in San Augustine and soon won Cornelia's heart. Colonel Price tried in vain to stop the romance, but his opposition only encouraged the couple's plan to elope to Louisiana and be married. One evening after dancing class, Fontaine and Cornelia slipped away in the Price family carriage, and headed to Gaines Ferry via *El Camino Real*. Cornelia's sisters rushed home to tell Colonel Price the unhappy news. Taking the family's remaining carriage, Price followed the fleeing couple, covering many miles until he reached Milam around midnight. The two lovers were speeding along *El Camino Real* and were nearing the ferry when Colonel Price caught up with them. He was just in time, for a light was shining in the ferryman's house and the couple would soon have been on the Louisiana side. Price ordered his daughter to return home and vented his wrath on the young Fontaine. Proud and hurt, the Frenchman went swiftly to the ferry to be rowed across, never to be seen again by the girl who so dearly loved him.

Cornelia was locked in her room for many days with only bread and water, but soon returned to her former life, though not so frivolous as before. In 1842 Cornelia married Charles R. Sossaman, and made him happy. The couple were parents of two boys and two girls. Sossaman died in 1859. The widowed Cornelia, still gracious and beautiful, married a second time in 1863 to General John G. Berry, a hero of the Cherokee War and prominent hotel owner in San Augustine. General Berry died in 1871 and Cornelia died not long afterward, probably in 1873. Many years ago, Price children playing in the field behind the old home place found a gold thimble with the name "Cornelia" engraved inside. Cornelia's story has become a legend in the Price family, as they imagine that she walked alone in the fields, remembering LeBlue Fontaine, her lost love.

San Augustine was first called the Ayish Bayou District, a large territory that extended south to present-day Jasper and Newton, east to the Sabine River, and north to include Shelby County and a part of Panola County. The entire district was part of a much larger area called the Department of Nacogdoches. San Augustine's location was advantageous, being about halfway between the Sabine River and Nacogdoches, situated astride *El Camino Real.*

In 1994, a Texas Highways article by Randy Mallory stated that "There are fifty-seven structures in San Augustine that bear Texas Historical Medallions; of these, six carry National Register of Historic Places designations." According to Marker Chairperson McXie Martin, as of 2006 additional historical designations have been added, making a total of seventy-five Texas markers and seven National designations.

William Seale in his narrative, *San Augustine in the Texas Republic*, states that "architecturally, the San Augustinians built an environment eminently superior to any town in Texas with the exception of Galveston– prior even to the Civil War. This was largely the contribution of master builder Augustus Phelps." [39]

Tragically, the youthful Phelps, who introduced Greek Revival architecture in San Augustine and East Texas, did not live to expand his talents elsewhere in Texas, as evidenced by his short obituary in *The Red Lander* on September 23, 1841: "Died in this city on the 22nd inst., Mr. Augustus Phelps, aged 23 years."

The Ezekiel Cullen Home, San Augustine, Texas 1839
Designed by Master Builder Augustus Phelps

San Augustine: A Texas Treasure, published in 2001 by the East Texas Historical Association, describes the life and times of this historic community in greater detail that the constraints of space allow us in this chapter.

El Camino Real from San Augustine to Nacogdoches: A Surveyor's Perspective

One of our most interesting and comprehensive interviews was with A.E. (Jake) Whitton, San Augustine County Surveyor for the past 38 years. His office is located in the old Whitton family home, a large two-story Victorian edifice bearing the distinction of being the first house in San Augustine with indoor plumbing. Throughout the years Jake has surveyed much of the land adjoining the Old Camino Trace in East Texas, and his knowledge is of encyclopedic proportions. He spoke of his uncle, W.N. Whitton, his predecessor as County Surveyor. Uncle Newt died at 102 years of age, leaving behind an abundance of maps and documents pertaining to the Old Road. A visit with Jake Whitton gives a person the desire to learn more. Now, when traveling down Highway 21 toward Nacogdoches, we often think of how illuminating it would be if sections of the original unpaved roadbed were properly marked, allowing modern-day travelers the opportunity to see *El Camino Real* in much the same way as the early pioneers.

Milton Garrett home, c. 1829, faces Highway 21 near San Augustine, Texas. The restoration by Raiford Stripling retained original features of the early home, including bullet holes from skirmishes during Republic of Texas days.

The Attoyac River

Heading westward from San Augustine, the traveler along El Camino Real passes through the little hamlet of Denning, and by the 1826 frontier home of Milton Garrett before crossing the Attoyac River, boundary line between Nacogdoches and San Augustine counties. The river derived its name from the Attoyac Indians, who lived along its banks and in its humus-rich bottomlands centuries ago. According to historian Ralph Smith, in November 1823 Alexander Horton's family chose the eighty-acre "island" on the Attoyac River for their first home in East Texas, an area associated with Gil Y'Barbo and his son-in-law, Juan Ignacio Guerrero, before 1800. Smith wrote:

> Little time or labor was required for them to build a cabin. They let pine boards, held in place by pine poles, serve as a covering; they hung a clapboard door on wooden hinges, and built a wide stick and dirt chimney to give the structure the characteristics of a house. The bare earth served as the floor, and pine logs placed against the

outside walls served to keep predatory animals from burrowing under the ground and entering the cabin....The young frontiersman (Horton) often killed deer from the cabin door....Horton's mother Susanna did not like the location because it was too far from human habitation. She wanted to move out upon the Redlands, where there were settlers and a school for the children." [40]

A story often related by the late Kirby Smith centered around his family's journey from Nacogdoches to San Augustine in 1911. The travelers included Henry and Alice Smith, their children, and all four grandparents. The family's three wagons were laden with all their worldly possessions as they set out along *El Camino Real* for the three-day, two-night trip. The first night was spent near the Melrose settlement, and the second night at the common campground on the Attoyac River. They slept under the wagons to protect themselves from the morning dew. The old wooden bridge on the Attoyac was flooded due to heavy rains, and the horses refused to cross. Covering the horses' eyes with handkerchiefs, the men were able to coax and lead them through the water to the river's east bank.

By 1918 the family owned the Smith Lake property, where Henry Smith became one of San Augustine County's best farmers. He introduced rotational crop management to the area, and in the 1920s and 1930s was recognized by Texas A&M and the State of Texas for his superior farming techniques.

The Attoyac River between San Augustine and Nacogdoches county line

Chireno

Today's Highway 21 straightens out the original *Camino Real* route through downtown Chireno, although some people still like to make the slight detour and take the old way down Gingerbread Lane. There's a special feeling of being in touch with generations of good and friendly people, just driving through. The late Miss Pearl Travis was a writer for the *Redland Herald* for many years. Excerpts from her history of Chireno deserve to be shared...

"Jose Antonio Chirino, a native of Spain for whom the village of Chireno received its name, had been given a grant of nine leagues of land (almost 40,000 acres) in 1792 and was living in the Chireno area before 1824 when a Mexican Constitution included a provision inviting colonists into Texas. His tract of land was located between the Attoyac and Angelina Rivers, bounded on the northeast by the right bank of Amaladeros Creek.

"Calvin Fall, the oldest son of Dr. J.N. Fall, is said to have been the first white child born in Chireno in 1840. The Indians were curious to see a white baby and were allowed to rock the cradle when they came to see him.

"Following Texas independence from Mexico in 1836, many colonists came from the United States. However, it was not until after the Civil War in the late 1860's and early 1870's that so many came from the broken South to Texas where they hoped to begin life all over again...Good camping places where water was available were vital for these wagon trains and horseback riders, and the little stretch of level land with its shade trees...formed an inviting stopping place for weary travelers.

"What had been the King's Highway or Royal Road when Texas was a colony of Spain became the Gateway to Texas as immigrants literally poured in from the United States. It was about forty miles between the towns of San Augustine and Nacogdoches where supplies could be purchased. Travel by horse or mule averaged about twenty miles a day, so Chireno almost had to be a stopping place. A stagecoach inn, called Halfway House because it was mid-point between the two old settlements, was built at Chireno in 1841 and served patriots of the Republic and later the State of Texas as a popular center for travelers until railways came in the late 1800's."[41]

The Halfway House, also known by names of previous owners Flournoy and Granberry, is a "two-story I-house, or saddlebags type, hewn-log dwelling with square notch corner joists. It is two rooms wide and one room deep with a dogtrot or central hall....the significance of the house is derived from its architecture, its association with prominent early settlers, and its service to the Chireno area as an early post office. Samuel Flournoy was the postmaster beginning in 1843. The mail route went from Crocket to San Augustine via Master's, Mount Airy, Douglass, Nacogdoches, Melrose, Flournoy's property and on to San Augustine." [42]

Halfway House is now owned by the Chireno Historical Society and has been completely restored. In 1994 the organization published *Memories of Chireno* through the combined efforts of Willie Thorp, Alton and Letitia Holt, Walt Roberts, Brooksie Kennemer, Reginald and Kaye Monzingo, and contributing citizens.

The Halfway House, Chireno, Texas

Two points of interest deserve to be mentioned in Chireno: The first oil well discovered in Texas in 1867 at Oil Springs produced oil for a few years and earlier provided oil for the wheels of pioneer wagons. The old tan-yards that once produced saddles, boots, shoes, and other leather goods is a unique site to visit as well.

Melrose

Melrose was established in 1841 when property for the community, its churches and schools was given by Dr. T.J. Johnson and his wife. Melrose once was home to three gins, three retail stores, a post office, dentist office, doctor's office, and was known as The Domino Capital of East Texas. Today, the pictorial history and southern style hospitality of Melrose is kept alive by the friendliness and good food of Carl and Nelda Dyes. Their restaurant, Dye's Kountry Katfish, is filled with pictures and mementoes of times past in Melrose, from pond baptizings to horse drawn carriages.

Long ago life in Melrose was quite lively, as evidenced by an article in *The Red Lander* dated October 28, 1841:

"In the vicinity of Melrose on Friday Evening, the 22nd, inst., by the Hon'l Wm. Hart, Dr. T. Jeff Johnson to Miss Amanda Engledow, all of Nacogdoches County. P.S. To the members of the Marrying Club in San Augustine: Wedding cake is the order of the day about Melrose–and girls are plenty–boys come over!" [43]

Nacogdoches: Following the Red Brick Road

Nacogdoches is an amazing and unique city whose residents are blessed with an innate ability to look forward, and backward, simultaneously. Nacogdoches in 2006 is growing, thriving and reaching out toward new levels of economic development and educational excellence. At the same time, its unequaled significance in the history and heritage of Texas is remembered, respected and promoted with a constancy not seen in many other areas of our state. It is as if there is an unseen "joining of hands" in Nacogdoches, its citizens realizing that an appreciation of their city's diverse and illustrious past is an important foundation for their future.

In 1936 the Texas Highway Department printed "A Guide to Points of General Interest in Division No. 11" in honor of our state's Centennial Celebration. The East Texas counties along *El Camino Real* were a major focus of their booklet. Interestingly, many of the locales mentioned seventy years ago are still important to us.

In the section on Nacogdoches County, the reader in 1936 was reminded that "Nacogdoches played an important part in the freeing of Texas. It was here that the smouldering flames of unrest were fanned into the rebellion that led to the independence of Texas."[44] The Texas Highway publication continued:

"North Street, *Calle de Norte*, could certainly be classified as the oldest street in Texas; the dusty, well-traveled road leading to the Nasonite Indian settlement. 'This has always been the principal residence street of Nacogdoches; the homes of such great men of Texas as General Thomas J. Rusk and Judge Charles S. Taylor... Such notable people as Captain Gil Y'Barbo, Sam Houston, James Bowie, and David Crockett have left their footprints on this famous old street...its companion is Main Street, called *La Calle Principal* by the Spaniards.' This is the familiar 'red brick road,' the original route of *El Camino Real* winding its busy way through the heart of downtown Nacogdoches.

"*The Old Stone Fort* has a history more intriguing, more romantic, than any building in Texas, including the Alamo. Over the walls of the 'stone house' have flown eight flags...the royal flag of Spain, the flag of the Magee-Gutierrez expedition of 1813, that of Dr. James Long's Republic of 1819, the flag of the Republic of Fredonia of 1826, the Mexican flag, the Lone Star flag of the Texas Republic, the Stars and Bars of the Confederacy, and the Stars and Stripes.

"The stone house was built as a private enterprise by Captain Gil Y'Barbo in 1779, and as a trading post it became the most important building in the New Philippines. Cordero, Governor of the Province of Texas, and General Herrera, with 1300 Spanish troops had headquarters in the stone house when, on November 6, 1806, the treaty was signed which averted war between Spain and the United States. In 1801 Peter Ellis Bean and the remainder of Philip Nolan's expedition were imprisoned in the old Stone Fort, where they remained for thirty days. For three months it was the seat of government of the Eastern Provinces of Spain, when Governor Manuel de Salcedo was in Nacogdoches during the summer of 1810.

"The first two newspapers to be published in Texas were printed in the old Stone Fort. It again became the seat of government when it was seized by the Fredonians in 1826. Following the collapse of the Fredonian Republic, the building was occupied as a home by John Durst, who sold it to Juan Hora, the district judge, and Vincente Cordova, who was district attorney under the Mexican regime. The official records were again placed in the old building, where they remained until a courthouse was built in 1840. In 1840 it was transferred to Rebecca Fenley, a daughter of Mrs. John S. Roberts. In 1901 it was purchased by Perkins Brothers, and demolished.

"This old building originally stood on the corner of Main and Fredonia Streets, facing the northeast corner of Plaza Principal, where the two main branches of *El Camino Real* merged. It was rebuilt in 1902 on the northwest corner of the Nacogdoches High School campus, where it is now being used as a library and museum." [45]

There is, of course, another chapter to the Old Stone Fort story. It resides today on the campus of Stephen F. Austin State University, accurately restored and preserved as an historical museum of the first order. It remains the landmark "anchor" for Nacogdoches and all of East Texas. A marker commemorating the life of Stephen F. Austin, "Father of Texas," has been placed in front of the Old Stone Fort by the Sons of the Republic of Texas. Articles from local newspapers published in the mid-1800's provide insightful looks into Nacogdoches events during those times:

From the *Nacogdoches Times*, December 9, 1848:
"Our District Court adjourned over from Saturday, December 2nd, to next Monday one week. The adjournment was urged upon the Court by the whole bar, and pretty much all the jurymen and witnesses. The fact was, all were worried out by the cold rain and unpleasant weather, the absence of any preparation for warming the Court House, and the impossibility of getting witnesses to attend in such stormy seasons. 'His Honor' therefore adjourned for a week, no doubt hoping that the weather would finish its 'blow out' and behave decently. This week, we regret to say, it has acted for some time in a 'most violent and outrageous manner: first it blew, then it snew, then it thaad, and then it friz horrid.' We have had cold weather enough for an army of Sons of Temperance..."

From the *Nacogdoches Times*, June 3, 1848:
"The New Catholic Church: As if by magic, a modest and symmetrical little church, dressed in white and green, with its neat cupola and pillars without, organ gallery and other suitable fittings within, has in the last few months raised its head in our little village, through the enterprising zeal of two French gentlemen of the clerical profession, from France. This church, we learn, will be consecrated the 11th instant, services be commenced at 9 o'clock a.m., and a Catholic clergyman from Galveston be in attendance."

From the *Red Lander*, September 9, 1841:

"The good citizens of Nacogdoches are making some praise-worthy exertions to encourage the business of education among the rising generation. Many excellent schools are in operation in different parts of the county, and the zeal and ability of some of their preceptors is well worthy the commendation and patronage of parents and guardians."

From the *Nacogdoches Times*, August 4, 1849:

"Mr. Hobart is still at the Planter's Hotel, taking Daguerreotypes in a style superior to any that have been taken heretofore in this place. He will remain a week longer, affording opportunity to those of the vicinity who wish correct likenesses, to obtain them."

From the *Nacogdoches Chronicle*, October 8, 1852:

"We hope our hotel keepers and merchants will bear in mind that the Grand Lodge of Texas (Masonic) meets in this place in January next, and that it will be necessary to have plenty to eat, and good, comfortable rooms, with fireplaces or stoves in them, enough to accommodate three or four hundred persons. Every intelligent citizen of the place would, of course, be mortified and crestfallen should a number of persons visit our town and be unable to get comfortable quarters...We are well aware of one thing, that Nacogdoches can do such things up 'brown,' and we hope she will outdo herself, even in this instance."

From the *Nacogdoches Chronicle*, October 16, 1852:

"The mail is now carried in handsome two-horse coaches three times a week between this place (Nacogdoches) and Henderson."

From the *Nacogdoches Chronicle*, November 23, 1852:

"The First Three Hundred Families: Of this illustrious band of pioneers and patriots introduced into the province of Texas by Gen. Stephen F. Austin, only nineteen heads of families are now remaining."

From the *Nacogdoches Chronicle*, June 14, 1853:

"Gen. Sam Houston will address the people of Nacogdoches, at the Court House, this afternoon, at two o'clock. The 'Old Hero' is in fine health and spirits, and our citizens may expect to be entertained in his usual happy manner."

From the *Nacogdoches Chronicle*, September 6, 1853:

"Expedition: J.C. Harrison, Esq., the editor of this paper, accompanied Gen. Rusk on the expedition to El Paso. He has been suffering from ill health some months, and goes to snuff the fresh breeze of the prairies as a remedy. We hope to see him back, renewed in mental and physical energy in a few months." [46]

A major jewel of Nacogdoches is Stephen F. Austin State University. Interestingly, its location was a part of the land settled by Pedro Padilla, whose daughter Maria became the wife of Gil Y'Barbo. The property was later owned by Thomas J. Rusk. In 1998 the Daily Sentinel published an account of the College's founding years by Regents Professor of History Jere Jackson. Its charter year was 1917, with the construction of Stephen F. Austin State Teachers College beginning in 1921. The first school semester was in 1923.

The driving force in the establishment of the college in Nacogdoches was Ira Link Sturdevant, described by Professor Jackson as follows:

"Ira Link Sturdevant, always known as 'Capt. Sturdevant,' from his days with the Stone Fort Rifles, was the President and later Chairman of the Board of Stone Fort Bank. Born in 1857, he died in 1953. He was one of the most influential men in the early part of the 20th century in Nacogdoches. Without the vision of Sturdevant and his attention to progressive ideas, the 'modern' aspects touted in the TWENTY THREE REASONS WHY (...The Stephen F. Austin State Normal ought to be located at Nacogdoches) would not have existed in Nacogdoches: the water system, the telephone, the fire department, and especially electricity. Sturdevant, a collector of fine books, also wanted a college for his town for intellectual reasons." [47]

Words alone cannot express the gratitude citizens of Nacogdoches should and must feel for the early chroniclers of its history such as R.B. Blake and George L. Crocket. Their meticulous approach to historical accuracy has continued in recent years through the competent endeavors of people like Dr. Archie McDonald, Dr. F.E. Abernethy, Joe and Carolyn Ericson, and the late Lucille Fain of the *Daily Sentinel's* Heritage Series.

Nacogdoches, actually, is a whole history book in itself. Many of the above historians, and others, have written prolifically about its past, and the men and women who walked its streets. There are so many persons, both famous and infamous, who have made East Texas and Nacogdoches what they are today. Many now lie in the historic Oak Grove Cemetery and other burial sites throughout Nacogdoches County. In this brief narrative, we have barely touched the "tip of the iceberg" in regard to historic Nacogdoches. There is so much more to tell...

Stephen F. Austin statue located on the campus of
Stephen F. Austin State University

Historic Oak Grove Cemetery, Nacogdoches, Texas

Influential soldier and statesman Thomas J. Rusk (1803-1857) came to Texas in 1834, signed the Texas Declaration of Independence in 1836 as a delegate from Nacogdoches, and chaired the committee to revise the Constitution. Rusk bravely fought in the Battle of San Jacinto on April 21, 1836. President Sam Houston appointed Rusk Secretary of War in his first Administration. In 1841, Rusk, J. Pinckney Henderson, and Kenneth L. Anderson formed the most famous law firm of that time in Texas. In 1845 Rusk helped establish Nacogdoches University, serving as President in 1846, during Republic of Texas days.

Thomas J. Rusk Statue, downtown Nacogdoches

Old Nacogdoches University Building, Nacogdoches, Texas

Douglass

The little village of Douglass sits prominently on *El Camino Real*, fourteen miles from Nacogdoches and eleven miles from Alto. It was established in 1836 by Michael Costley on an 800-acre tract of land purchased from John Durst, who had come to Texas with his brothers Joseph and Jacob Durst in the early 1800's, entering by way of Natchitoches and *El Camino Real*. Costley named his newly-purchased settlement Douglass in honor of a man he admired named Kelsey Harris Douglass, owner of a mercantile business in Nacogdoches during the struggle for Texas independence. Douglass sold large orders of dry goods to the Texas army during the crucial months of the Revolution, then represented Nacogdoches County in the Second Congress.

Costley expected the little village to flourish. It was the site of a stagecoach inn which was a stop-over between San Antonio and Nacogdoches. Horses for the stage coaches were often changed there. The first mercantile business in Douglass was Costley and Ables. Over the years Douglass has had several stores: a drugstore, blacksmith shop, a few saloons, hotel and boarding house, and two cotton gins. The Douglass Post Office was chartered by the Republic of Texas in 1836, then became a U.S. Post office in 1846. From 1861 until the end of the Civil War it was a Confederate Post Office.

We traveled over to Douglass at the suggestion of our Indian writer Lila Kerr (Chapter One) to visit the Douglass Independent School District library. Beginning in 1976 and for nearly twenty years following, a bi-yearly publication called *The Chinquapin* was published by students and teachers in the Douglass High School. The history students interviewed early residents of the area, recorded and transcribed their recollections, took pictures of their subjects and the Douglass environs, and printed issues in the Fall and Spring semesters of the school year. Copies of *The Chinquapin* are still available from the beginning issue in 1976, and can be purchased for $5.00 each from the Douglass ISD office.

Alto

The community of Alto in Cherokee County was named at the suggestion of Captain Henry Berryman because the proposed site was situated on a high dividing ridge between the Neches and Angelina Rivers. Thus, the name "Alto," meaning *high*, became the name of this settlement with *El Camino Real* as its main artery of transportation from the earliest days. Cherokee County, of which Alto is a part, was organized in 1846, with the town of Alto founded in 1849. "The community is situated on a part of the old Barr and Davenport land grant which was made to them in 1798. These men died before claiming possession, and the property was conveyed to John Durst, who had accumulated large tracts of land as payment for his services as interpreter for the Mexican government among the Indians. The Barr and Davenport grant encompassed nearly 42,000 acres. Over time, hundreds of farms have been sold from this vast tract of land." [48]

In 1936 the *Alto Herald* issued a small booklet in connection with the Texas 100th Centennial Celebration. This publication gives an excellent account of the early days of Alto and some of its first residents:

> "Mrs. John Durst in her "Memoirs of Early Days" gives us a splendid picture of conditions in East Texas from 1835 to 1839. John Durst fled from Monclova, Coahuila, where he was attending a session of the Texas-Coahuila Legislature in 1835, coming to Alto to warn the people of the approach of Santa Anna. He covered the distance of 965 miles in twelve days, and on the same horse! John Durst built two strong block houses and connected them with a stockade which surrounded his home. He also had a secret cellar dug beneath his residence. All these were used as a means of protection for his family, friends and neighbors. Mrs. Durst said that sometimes all available space was filled with refugees." [49]

The old town of Linwood, near Alto, was known originally as the town of Angelina, because it was near the river, and was the head of navigation for boats making regular trips up and down the Angelina carrying freight and passengers. The old Selman graveyard in Linwood is possibly the oldest Anglo-American cemetery in Cherokee County. It is the final resting place for many pioneer families. Candace Bean, wife of Peter Ellis Bean, was buried there in 1848.

Weches

The community of Weches, founded about 1847, is close to the site of the *San Francisco de los Tejas Mission*. Its founder, T.J. Hennin, named the settlement Neches for its proximity to the Neches River. Its first post office in 1847-48 was called Neches. From 1853-1882 the community was called Naches. By 1887 the time had come to apply for a new post office. Finding that their chosen name, Neches, was already taken by another community, they changed the name to Weches. The peak population for Weches was about 400 as late as 1920. Before 1900 the town had a steam gristmill, cotton gin, general store, and a Baptist church. A few years later a Methodist church and Church of Christ were added. Today, there are no businesses remaining in Weches, and less than thirty residents. However, there is still an active post office.

Crockett

A pleasant drive over to Crockett one sunny afternoon reminded us once again of the natural beauty of East Texas along *El Camino Real*. Highway 21 is a seemingly wider road between Alto and Crockett, perhaps because, unlike deeper East Texas, it traverses areas of open pastureland. The historic markers along the way are visible and well-maintained. Much of this is due, at least in part, to the reason for our trip: we were on our way to interview a legend in Houston County: Eliza Bishop, historian extraordinaire and Marker Chairperson of the Houston County Historical Commission. As of 2006, there are nearly 300 historical markers and designations in Houston County, most of which are due to the perseverance and painstaking diligence of Eliza Bishop. We spent several leisurely, enjoyable hours visiting with this fountain of knowledge who wrote articles for both the *Houston Post* and *Houston Chronicle* for years, and still writes on occasion. She put together a "mini-tour" leaflet for tourists and visitors as a means of promoting Crockett and all its positive attributes, most of which center around the people coming together "as one" for progress.

Davy Crockett Spring in downtown Crockett, Texas

In 1837, Houston County became the first county created and organized in Texas. Crockett, the county seat, was nothing more than a small village during the struggle for Texas independence. David Crockett stopped there on his way to the Alamo, and camped under a large oak tree near a spring about five hundred feet from the main square of the present town. Both the oak tree and the spring carry the name of Davy Crockett. As of 2006, a sightseeing park is being established on East Goliad Street near the newly restored depot. Upon completion, "Davy Crockett Spring Park" will be dedicated, featuring the six flags that have flown over Texas, as well as a simulated log cabin.

On July 29, 2006, the 1909 Missouri Pacific Railroad building (the Old Depot) was dedicated as the *Houston County Visitors Center and Museum*. The Old Depot, a stopping place for passenger and freight trains, has been completely restored and adapted for its new use.

Down on Camp Street there is the bronze statue of Sam Lightnin' Hopkins, "a bluesman who played in the establishments along Camp Street when it was the center of the black business district around 1940. From Camp Street to Carnegie Hall, Hopkins influenced musicians around the world."... words on the plaque under his statue. Today, Guy and Pipp Gillette operate a live entertainment hall called "The Camp Street Cafe."

As we left Eliza Bishop that day, she remarked, "Remember, anything worth doing is worth doing 'write'!" Sage advice from a very wise lady... we thought to ourselves..."Yes, how very true...history unrecorded is history lost."

Austonio

Austonio's first name was Pearville. According to Eliza Bishop, the community, located on *El Camino Real* fourteen miles west of Crockett, was established before 1900. By 1930 the citizens decided that a new name was needed, and held a contest for that purpose. "The winning entry came from Ruth Tucker, who suggested the name Austonio, a combination of Austin and San Antonio."

By 1931 there was a consolidated school and a post office. By 1940 the population had reached its high of 150, and there were four stores. By 1964 the school had consolidated with Lovelady, and the post office closed in 1971. The 2000 census reported the population of Austonio at thirty-seven.

The Trinity River

Our journey through East Texas by way of *El Camino Real* concludes at the eastern bank of the Trinity River. The twisting, winding, historic stream claims the honor of being the longest river lying entirely in Texas, with a watershed covering nearly 18,000 square miles. The Caddo Indians called it Arkikosa; La Salle called it River of the Canoes in 1687; Domingo Teran called the same river Encarnacion de Verbo in 1691. By 1716 it had been given its permanent name, "the Trinity," so called by Domingo Ramon, the Marques de Aguayo, and many later Spaniards. Much like the Sabine in many respects, the Trinity's snags, sand bars and seasons of low water impeded river traffic. Even so, about 1836 numerous boats began steaming up the Trinity River, bringing groceries and dry goods and carrying down cotton, sugar, cowhides, and deer skins. The steam-boat era gave way to transport by rail during the early 1870's.

The *Nacogdoches Chronicle* on November 8, 1853 reported the following:

> "Steam Ship: Two of our most social and enterprising citizens left us during the past week in the persons of Messrs. Bondies and Rohte, the former the Captain and latter the Clerk of the steamer *Kate*. They go to take command of her and will commence business immediately on their arrival. She will make regular trips from Magnolia on the Trinity to Galveston. As a good humored, whole-souled gentleman, the Captain is beyond our commendation. As for Mr. Rohte, we can say on the score of personal acquaintance and attachment that his warm heart and generous qualities will continue to make a favorite on the river. No *Kate* could be in better hands." [50]

Claudia Wilbarger Norvell. *Sketch by Richard Murphy*

Chapter Nine

Saving The Road

A Tribute to
Mrs. Lipscomb (Claudia Wilbarger) Norvell
(1880 -1962)

It was the year 1911. Passage of the 19th Amendment to the United States Constitution was several years away. Women's Rights, including the vote, were yet to be achieved in Texas and most other parts of the nation. During that same year, however, there was a young Texas woman of most remarkable talents named Claudia Norvell who determined that the King's Highway, *El Camino Real*, must be saved from oblivion, no matter how monumental the task. Neither timid nor fearful, she became the driving force in successfully persuading both the powerful and the prestigious to join her cause. Her own words, penned in the introduction to her 1945 book, tell the story best:

> "When I was a child of eight in Bastrop, Texas, a friend of my father's, a plantation owner, would invite of my mother two children to spend the weekend with his little girls. In the three-seated hack I always sat in front, by the captain, and was given the reins of the horses to hold.
>
> "In crossing the Colorado River at Bastrop, I remember so well his pointing out to me a deep ravine in the bank, running into the river and stating to me, 'That was the old King's Highway across Texas.' The ravine was the roadway made by the burro's hook-claws pulling up the bank when loaded with great sacks of metals and goods. He pictured this royal highway running from Mexico to Natchitoches, Louisiana. And when I was grown, visiting in Eastern Texas, there I found more of this King's Highway. I decided then that this highway must be made alive again.
>
> "In attending my first Congress of the Daughters of the American Revolution, April, 1911, in Washington, DC, I became very much interested in the reports of the *Old Trails Roads of America*; roads blazed through the wilderness across the great divide. Burnes Lick Road, the Wilderness Road and the Oregon

Trail were called the civilization roads of the United States. The Santa Fe trail had just been surveyed and marked with monuments. Miss Elizabeth Butler Gentry of Missouri stated the Santa Fe Trail had been blazed by William Beckwell in 1848, and was the oldest trail in America.

"Then the thought came to me that Texas had a much older road—some two hundred years older. As delegate from my Texas chapter, I arose and asked for a special privilege—to speak for Texas. Permission was granted and after I spoke Texas was added to the Old Trails Roads, Daughters of the American Revolution, memorializing *El Camino Real*, the Old San Antonio Road to the pioneers of Texas.

"In Texas, we have a strategic military highway across the State ordered by the King of Spain in 1691: a road was to be found to the Eastern Indians, a highway of international importance, a constant and dominant factor that became the scene of direct and continued competition between France and Spain for control of the Texas Empire. It connected famous trading sites, Missions and Forts across Texas and Louisiana, traversing Texas counties from the Sabine River to the Rio Grande.

"I have studied King's Highway, and for many years have engaged in the work of its perpetuation, conserving its outlines to memorialize the pioneers of Texas, by erecting monuments and by paving the highway across the State. To what degree I have succeeded, the public must judge. In every event I have done my best, and have no excuse to offer. After many years I have achieved my goal. I love Texas, and the work has been a joy to me." [51]

Claudia Norvell was made Texas Chairman of the National Old Trails and Roads Committee of the DAR in November 1911. Marking of King's Highway, *El Camino Real*, was to be accomplished by placing boulders of Texas pink granite along the trail, five miles apart, at the crossroads and boundary lines of counties, from the Sabine River to Mexico. The monuments were to be five feet in height, three and one-half feet by two and one-half feet in width, at a cost of $28.00 each. Subscriptions for the markers and private donations would be welcomed, but it was felt that the State should pay for surveying the trail.

With her organization's enthusiastic backing, Mrs. Norvell approached the Texas Legislature with a funding request to survey and mark King's Highway. In February 1913 House Bill #290 would have appropriated $5,000 (more if necessary) in general revenue funds for the project, but it was vetoed by Governor Oscar B. Colquitt. Undaunted, over the next two years Mrs. Norvell used her considerable powers of persuasion to convince legislators, historians, educators and citizens that saving the ancient trail was of ultimate importance, and simply had to be done. By 1915-16 she was knocking once again on the doors of the State Capitol, this time armed with an accurately rendered map of *El Camino Real* prepared by the University of Texas' esteemed Spanish archivist W. E. Dunn.

The Texas State Historical Association had been contacted by Mrs. Norvell in August 1914, asking for guidance in selecting a qualified scholar to make the map. After consulting on her behalf with Dr. Eugene C. Barker of the University of Texas, TSHA's Charles W. Ramsdell suggested obtaining the services of Professor Dunn, a noted historian "thoroughly conversant with that period." Mr. Ramsdell further commented, "I think you are well on the way towards accomplishing your cherished object, and I believe that not only historical students, but the whole State of Texas will owe you a vote of thanks."

In November 1914 Professor Dunn was employed by Mrs. Norvell for a sum of $400.00. He was requested to "make a correct map of the *Camino Real* that we can give to a surveyor and can be traced on the land to know just where the old road did run...from the Sabine River to the Rio Grande River." Professor Dunn spent several months of intensive study in locating the exact route, researching old land grants and field notes at the General Land Office in Austin. Time was also spent in the libraries of Washington, D.C. and New York. The original trail from the Sabine River to San Antonio was determined with certainty using the substantial documentation available. However, the road from San Antonio to the Rio Grande River posed a problem, due to a lack of records and the fact that in many long stretches it had simply disappeared. Fortunately, the 1778 Diary kept by the Explorer-Chaplain Morfi when accompanying the Croix Expedition from Mexico to San Antonio provided an accurate description of this southern part of the road, allowing Professor Dunn to complete his map. In 1915 his findings were further confirmed during a trip to Spain. In November 1916 he wrote Mrs. Norvell: "I found a new map of this expedition in Spain last year which shows the old road. It does not change any of my previous findings, but, indeed, strengthens them."

In 1916, a bill presented by Senator Louis J. Wortham was passed "to pay the cost of surveying and establishing the Old San Antonio Road, sometime referred to as *King's Highway–Camino Real*, from the point where the same crosses the boundary between Texas and Louisiana to be expended by the Governor for the surveying of the road by Dr. W.E. Dunn's map of road prepared as an archivist. Appropriation: $5,000." A later bill appropriated an additional $3,000 for marking the trail. Governor James E. Ferguson appointed Major V.N. Zivley to survey The Road.

Mrs. Norvell and the Texas DAR members raised $10,544.00 for the *King's Highway/Camino Real* project, to which was added the State's $8,000.00. In December 1917 the contract for 123 granite markers was let at Austin to A.L. Gooch Granite and Limestone Company for $4,300.00, and signed by Governor Hobby, A.L. Gooch, and Mrs. Lipscomb Norvell. Judge Hiram Glass secured a half-rate from the railroads for transporting the markers to all the counties in which they would be erected.

No doubt the major emphasis placed on the surveying and marking of King's Highway made quite a positive impression on the members of the Texas Legislature, and caused them to take a fresh new look at the existing roads throughout the State. Years later, Mrs. Norvell's recollections concerning the passage of the 1916 King's Highway Bill are an interesting addition to the story: "When the Bill was passed, a representative (George B. Terrell of Linwood/Alto) from Cherokee County said, 'I am placing a Bill in the House for a State Highway Department, taking the roads out of the Post Office and the Agricultural Departments.' Before the King's Highway-*Camino Real* Bill, little attention was given to the building of permanent highways in the State." [52]

Thus, by 1917 the Texas State Highway Department was organized as a separate entity, and from that point forward our highways and roads throughout the State became a priority for both legislators and Texas citizens. Today, the thoroughfares all over Texas are among the safest and best in the Nation, thanks to the professionalism and expertise of the successor to that first Texas Highway Department, the Texas Department of Transportation, in building, managing and preserving our excellent system of roads.

Claudia Norvell's active involvement and unflagging zeal on behalf of *El Camino Real* continued for many years. On Texas Independence Day, March 2, 1920 the surveyed and marked trail was presented to the State of Texas during an impressive ceremony at San Pedro Park in San Antonio. In 1929 the historic road became the only highway created by Legislative Act, and its official name became "The Old San Antonio Road." The Act, spearheaded by former Texas Senator and then U.S. Congressman Nat Patton of Crockett, provided for a 100 foot right-of-way through the various counties affected by the road along its entire length. Congressman Patton was made President of the 20,000-member Old San Antonio Road Association, and Mrs. Lipscomb Norvell was named Honorary Life President.

By 1939, most of *El Camino Real*, Texas State Highway 21, was paved. That same year a large monument commemorating the 248th year of the Old San Antonio Road was erected at Normangee, Texas, accompanied by a celebration and dedicatory service. Included in the crowd of 3,000 were representatives from all the countries whose flags had flown over Texas. Stirring addresses were given by Rev. Paul J. Folk, Dr. Carlos E. Castenada, Dr. Eugene C. Barker, Hon. Clem F. Fain, Jr., and Judge R.N. Stripling, who was President of the Natchez-Natchitoches-Old San Antonio Road Parkway Association. The honor of unveiling the monument was given, of course, to Mrs. Lipscomb Norvell. An interesting list of guests at the reception following the ceremony included Col. Andrew Houston, son of General Sam Houston; and Misses Clara Driscoll and Adina De Zavala, the ladies credited most with saving the Alamo. Notables from East Texas included Mrs. Eugene Blount and J.L. Mock from Nacogdoches, Dr. C.W. Butler from Crockett, the Coles from Alto, the Phelans and Broussards from Beaumont, and Col. P.W. Downs from San Augustine. Sabine County was well represented by Mrs. R.S. Noble, E.H. Calloway, Clyde Russell, Max Mallory, Paul Rounsaville and R.W. Buce.

In 1945 Mrs. Norvell published a book entitled *King's Highway: The Great Strategic Military Highway*. Its pages are filled with personal letters, legal documents, legislative proceedings, newspaper clippings, old records, and an informative collection of historical data spanning her thirty-plus years of active involvement in preserving, surveying and marking *El Camino Real*. The volume was dedicated "To Texas and Her Centennial of Statehood. Behind the Road lies the Story of Civilization. It is the connecting link of what has gone before and of what is to be, and now it is fitting to dedicate to Texas, representing the Sovereignties under whose flags she has been, my work, The King's Highway–*El Camino Real*–Old San Antonio Road." [53]

In today's world we expect to see women of achievement and success in every profession and involved in promoting every worthy cause. They are applauded on every hand. But in 1911 times were quite different. Few women of that day ventured much past home, hearth, and family. Thus, it is refreshing to reflect on the story of Mrs. Lipscomb Norvell... Claudia Wilbarger Norvell...who in a unique, thoroughly amazing way...did both. She possessed qualities that enabled her to not only fulfill her family obligations, but save a famous old trail, already forgotten by many, that would surely have been lost without her perseverance. Claudia was mother to three children, Lipscomb, Jr., Margaret and Harvey. Her husband, Lipscomb, Sr. was in the wholesale hardware business. Her entire family was interested in, and supportive of, her efforts on behalf of *El Camino Real*, including her sister Annie (married to early lumberman John A. Gilbert) and her brother J.L. Wilbarger of Bastrop. And, as has been related, she was personable, knowledgeable and articulate, enlisting the aid of her sisters in the Texas Society, DAR to join her in saving the old trail. Being enterprising women of like mind, they gladly accepted the task.

In 1918, the year the granite markers were erected along *El Camino Real*, Claudia's son Lipscomb, Jr., then age 19 and a student at V.M.I. in Lexington, Virginia, registered for military service during World War I. In 1939, the year of the Celebration at Normangee, America was on the brink of involvement in World War II. During the war years, the early 1940s, *El Camino Real* was in frequent use as the access road across Texas for transporting military vehicles and soldiers to Fort Polk, Louisiana and points beyond. Certainly uppermost in Mrs. Norvell's mind was the fact that, as in its inception, the enduring old road was still "The Great Strategic Military Highway."

In March 1950, Texas Society DAR State Convention proceedings described an event at the Texas State Capitol held on February 21, 1950:

> "A signal honor has come to a Texas DAR. A portrait of Claudia Wilbarger Norvell (Mrs. Lipscomb) of Beaumont will hang in the Senate for all who visit there to honor her. She is the second Texas woman to be so honored, and the first DAR to be so recognized. *'Savior of El Camino Real, the Old Spanish Road of Texas Colonists, including 1,200 miles of the Old Spanish Trail through Texas'* is the caption of the name-plate under her portrait....The portrait is the work of Anthony Wills, noted artist of New York City. Mrs. W.B. Livesay was responsible for the promotion of this project. Senator W.R. Cousins supported by Representative Jack Brooks presented the bill in the Senate. $2,000 was donated through the Chapter by friends." [54]

Thus it was that *El Camino Real* achieved its rightful and significant place in Texas history, spearheaded by a woman who challenged others to catch her vision as well. Widowed in 1925, Claudia Norvell remained in Beaumont, Texas for the rest of her life. May we remember her always, and the lasting results she achieved for all of Texas.

A section of *El Camino Real*, reminiscent of
Mrs. Claudia Wilbarger Norvell's description of the King's Highway

Major V. N. Zively, C.E.
Sketch by Richard Murphy

Chapter Ten

*Surveying the Road
1915-1916*

Major V.N. Zivley, C.E., considered it imperative to keep Mrs. Claudia Norvell fully apprised as to the progress of his survey of King's Highway. His lengthy reports to her provided many personal glimpses into the arduous task to which he had been entrusted, and of the local citizenry's response as he painstakingly identified the correct route. Zively and his team of assistants began the survey at the eastern Gateway into Texas, Gaines Ferry on the Sabine River.

In his first report to Mrs. Norvell, dated December 6, 1915 from Normangee, Texas, he wrote:

> "I am availing myself of all the traditions as to location that are possible to obtain, but I always endeavor to verify the correctness of the traditions by something that is tangible and real, something that is of record, and that fixes the location as far back as the misty past.
>
> "I have indeed been fortunate in the character of assistance that has been given me in all the counties through which I have passed. In Sabine County, Mr. J.T. McGown at Pendleton's Ferry gave me invaluable aid, and at San Augustine, Mr. William Sharp, Mr. H.W. Sublett and Mr. A.E. Davis were active and enthusiastic in helping me. In San Augustine County there are three roads from the town of Milam to San Augustine, and there are good people living on each of these roads, who if need be would make affidavit that they are on the one and only *Camino Real*. Fortunately for me, there was in A.D. 1840 a lawsuit between Donald McDonald, administrator of the Quirk estate and Joseph Rowe et al. Ira P. Ellis was appointed by the District Court to re-survey and fix the southern boundary of the Quirk League, which was, and is, the King's Highway. Mr. A.E. Davis, a prominent attorney of San Augustine spent half a day helping me find the record of that work in the archives of the District

Court of San Augustine County, which enabled me to relocate the road with its every meander for a distance of nearly six miles.

"You must remember that seventy-five years ago it was comparatively easy to trace the road, while today in many places for miles and miles where the road has been abandoned and cultivated there is not the least evidence of its original location to be found on the ground.

"At Nacogdoches many of the citizens evinced the liveliest interest in the survey of the road, but I am especially indebted to Dr. J.E. Mayfield for his kindly courtesy and assistance. This venerable gentleman of the old Southern type has resided at Nacogdoches since 1848, except the four years he spent in the Confederate Army, and his knowledge of the location of the road through Nacogdoches County is perfect. He is as proud of Texas...her traditions, her history and institutions as anyone I have ever met, and it was indeed a treat to be with and hear him converse of the old settlers, and the notables that he had known in his youth and early manhood. With him I visited, measured and minutely examined the Old Stone Fort, and copied from its cornerstone this inscription:

THE STONE FORT
Built 1778   Re-erected 1907
By the Cum Concilio Club
to the memory
of those heroes whose courage rose superior to their
privations, and whose valor made possible
Texas Independence

"In Cherokee County, where John H. Reagan spent his first years in Texas, the citizens have proven their civic pride by maintaining the old road as a highway, almost in its original location, from the Angelina River on the East to the Neches River on the West. At Alto, two miles east of old Fort Terry, Mr. C.A. Harrison, a personal friend of General Sam Houston and Thomas J. Rusk, though cumbered with the weight and infirmities of many years, was especially helpful to me, and spent some time in riding with me over the road, pointing out the historic locations, and also showing me the initial corners of surveys made in the 'early thirties,' thus enabling me to verify by actual survey and measurement the correctness of the traditional location.

"In Houston County, from the Neches to the Trinity, the King's Highway has almost been abandoned and is obsolete. Of the fifty-seven miles running through that county less than fifteen miles of the original road is now used as a highway. Had it not been for the splendid and gratuitous assistance of Mr. J.H. Ellis, a former surveyor of that county who is familiar with the location of the old surveys which call for the road, my labor there would have been almost interminable. As it was I spent nearly a month in the county, in the most arduous work I have done in years, but have the satisfaction of knowing that I have relocated and marked the ancient highway.

"In this, Madison County, from the Trinity River to Normangee, only six miles of the old road is now used, but from Normangee to the Navasota River, about nine miles of the present road is almost identical with the original.

"Truly I have been surprised all along the route from the Sabine to the Navasota at the kindly and intelligent interest manifested in my work, and I have taken especial pains to antagonize no one... Nor have I ever failed to give you, Madam, all the credit for the initiation of the work. To your personal magnetism and your timely and persistent efforts, the State will ever be indebted for the re-survey and marking of the King's Highway, the road over and by which most of those immortal heroes of the Alamo and San Jacinto entered the State."

An editorial in the *Daily Sentinel* dated October 28, 1915 reflects the interest created with Major Zively's (called Captain in the newspaper) arrival in Nacogdoches.

"Capt. V.N. Zively, who is surveying the old King's Highway or San Antonio Road, arrived in the city Monday and put up a marker in front of the location of the Old Stone Fort. Capt. Zively tacked his marker on a telephone pole on Main Street but says he doubts that it is on the exact location of the old road where it once passed through our modern city. Tradition seems to indicate that the road traveled a course nearer where Pilar Street is now, which street got its name from an early church which was here before the Stone Fort was built.

"In tracing the road into Nacogdoches from the east Capt. Zively passed at a point about 100 feet north of where Mr. Gillette's silo stands, on down and across LaNana Creek about 300 feet north of the present Main Street bridge. He thinks that it would be very difficult to trace the road from the city on west until he gets out a distance of a few miles when he will be able to locate it almost exactly by old land surveys. The old land surveys have been one of the chief ways Capt. Zively has had of locating the road through Nacogdoches county and he has spent a considerable time gathering field notes in Hoya and Gilbert's office....An oak post marker is being set every five miles along the route marked 'King's Highway.' When the survey is completed the Daughters of the (American) Revolution will put up granite markers instead of the oak posts. As the posts are set they are also numbered. The marker in Nacogdoches is Number 16. Post 15 is east of the city on the upper Melrose road at a point near John Halton's place. 14 is five miles east of that, 500 yards south of the upper Melrose road in W.L. Dean's field."

By March 4, 1916 Major Zively was in San Antonio. His Second Report to Mrs. Norvell began as follows:

"Since then (referring to his First Report dated November, 1915 from Normangee) I have had some varied and unique experiences... (I) have passed through the finest agricultural and grazing land in the world, some of the most beautiful and picturesque country that ever delighted the eye of man, some of the blackest and most tenacious mud, and some of the longest and deepest stretches of sand in Texas...I have crossed three of the most prominent streams in the State: The Navasota, the Brazos and the Colorado...and also two others, the Rio San Marcos and Guadalupe...and (I) am now camped in the historic city near the far-famed San Pedro Springs."

Zively continued his narrative in minute detail, crediting County Commissioner Jacob Klaus and D.L. Horn, an old San Antonio settler described as possessing an infallible memory, with assistance in locating the trail through the city. Aware that some criticism of his surveyed route was occurring along the way, he felt compelled to assure Mrs. Norvell that..."I have no ax to grind, no piece of realty to be affected in value by its true location, no other object or end in view, that to do my work correctly, honestly and fearlessly."

It was the last leg of Major Zively's survey, from San Antonio to the Rio Grande, which "disheartened and almost discouraged" him most. In his final report he described traveling over "country so rough and broken that a wolf could hardly get over it." At one point he was twenty-five miles off-course and had to retrace his steps. Like Professor W.E. Dunn, whose map of the *Camino Real* route was his guide, Zively was grateful for the Morfi Diary. His assessment of that "learned and observant Spanish Priest who traveled the King's Highway in December 1778, from Presidio Rio Grande to the old Missions at San Antonio" was highly complimentary.

> "To that old Padre, though I am a Protestant of the most ultra blue stocking type, I want to doff my hat, as the most accurate artist in words of a country traversed that I have ever met--in books. Every place he mentioned, every object of interest, I found just as described by him in that brief Diary. His only inaccuracy was, in the distance stated between given points, invariably the distance given by him was greater than that of the steel tape. But I picture him as a scholarly, devout man of fragile physique, and wearied as he was by the day's travel, how natural for him to over-estimate distance."

There is no doubt that Major V.N. Zively, C.E. was the perfect choice for surveying the Road. Certainly his technical skills were noteworthy, but he also possessed a deep sensitivity to the subject being surveyed, as evidenced by his progressive reports of his work. In his final report, Zively expressed his thanks to all who had helped him along the way, and wrote:

> "It is a pleasure to state that having come in contact with people in every walk of life, and of various racial origin, from the Louisiana line to the border of Mexico, I met the kindest treatment from all,

and found them all intense in their love of Texas! Grand Old Texas! There is something about her red clay hills, her swamps and forests, her broad reaching prairies, her rugged mountains, and even her cactus covered roughs, that inspire the denizens of each locality with the belief that theirs is the most favored spot under heaven." [55]

A field of yellow spring flowers bordering *El Camino Real* near Milam, Texas

A section of *El Camino Real,* part of the Lobanillo Swales
near Geneva, Texas

Chapter Eleven

Locating the Markers

An Inscription Carved in Stone:

*KING'S HIGHWAY
CAMINO REAL
OLD SAN ANTONIO ROAD
MARKED BY THE
DAUGHTERS OF THE
AMERICAN REVOLUTION
AND THE STATE OF TEXAS
A.D. 1918*

By October 15, 1919, all 123 markers had been erected according to contract. Before making final payment for the stones, Mrs. Claudia Norvell sent letters to all County Judges in the counties along the King's Highway, asking them to inspect the monuments as "persons knowing all of the routes in their respective counties," making certain that all were properly installed and in place. Positive replies were received from all the Judges, and the project was deemed complete. Then in 1936, the Texas Society DAR made a decision to locate and rededicate as many of the markers as possible as a part of the Texas Centennial Celebration.

In 1998 the Texas Society DAR decided to make a concerted effort, both collectively and individually, to find, repair, document and rededicate these treasured monuments. Lisa Lee, DAR State Chairman for King's Highway Markers, contacted Kenneth Skillern, Chairman of the San Augustine County Historical Commission, asking for his assistance in locating and cataloguing the markers in the Eastern Texas region and beyond. As the subject was of particular interest to him, he agreed, accompanying Ms. Lee and her father, Jack Ward on a number of marker-locating expeditions.

During the seventy years since the 1936 inspection several of the monuments were moved to accommodate highway construction. Many had been abandoned as the road changed. During the tedious process of discovery, the three investigators located monuments in open pastureland and around the edges of forests. Some of the markers were even being used for such mundane purposes as the doorsteps to homes. And, due to the ravages of time, some of the inscribed granite slabs were toppled over, face down, in various locations so as to be hardly recognizable.

In our interview with Skillern he explained that although the granite markers were not numbered, the investigators used Major Zively's field notes which indicated numbered oak posts, number 1 being at the Sabine River, and so on. Thus, to assure accuracy they identified the markers by the same numbers. Interestingly, they found a marker at west Yegua Creek near Lincoln, Texas that was not shown on the surveyor's notes. It is located between markers 57 and 58. This extra marker, increasing the number to 124, is somewhat larger that the other 123, and has a slanted point on one side. The engraving is the same, however. How did this happen? Was this a prototype, not chosen because of its different size and shape? Or, since the marker at the Sabine River has the added line "Texas-Louisiana Border," did the contractor not count it with the 123? At any rate, in 1918 it was delivered to Lee County and installed in a visible location, although not five miles distant from the others.

When Lisa Lee was featured not long ago on the *Texas Country Reporter* television show, she commented on the markers still missing. Viewing the show that Sunday night was Billy Fussell of Milam, Texas, who called Lisa and said, "I know where # 5 is...My uncle Hogan Fussell showed it to me in 1973." Excitedly, Lisa called Mr. Skillern and asked him to investigate the find. He and Billy Fussell visited the site, but couldn't turn the heavy, nearly 1500-pound stone over to the inscription side until they returned with enough added strength to verify the discovery.

Kenneth Skillern describes how marker # 30 was found in Ike McKnight's front yard in Houston County by DAR member Wanda Siems: "As a child Ike and other neighborhood children played at a swimming hole about 400 yards from his present home. He remembered a big rock lying on the bank of the creek, and decided to bring it to his house with the help of his three sons. They loaded the monument onto the upturned hood of an old car and skidded it home. Upon turning it over, they discovered the inscription. Carefully, meticulously they cleaned the stone, and today it stands proudly in front of Mr. McKnight's house on Texas Highway 21, about 8 miles west of Crockett."

As of 2006 most all the 1918 pink granite markers have been located. However, there are still eleven monuments missing, as follows: # 13, Nacogdoches County; #19, west bank of the Angelina River; # 39, Madison County; # 49, Burleson County; # 68, Bastrop County; and # 69, Caldwell County; all of which are on Highway 21. The other five missing markers are located on ranch land near the Texas/Mexico border. They are # 100 and # 113, La Salle County; # 120, Dimmitt County; # 121 and # 122, Maverick County. It is hoped that watchful Texas citizens will continue to assist in locating the last few undiscovered monuments so that they may be returned to their original sites.

An East Texas trail through the woods

These highway signs appear at intervals along Texas Highway 21

Chapter Twelve

*El Camino Real Real de los Tejas National Historic Trail
Recognition at Last!*

On October 18, 2004 when President George W. Bush signed legislation naming *El Camino Real de los Tejas* a National Historic Trail, the ancient, multiple-route roadway gained the nationwide recognition it has long deserved. Only fifteen other Historic Trails throughout America have been so designated since the National Trails Act was enacted in 1968. Joining the prestigious company of famous National Trails such as Lewis and Clark, Mormon Pioneer, Pony Express, Oregon, Santa Fe, Trail of Tears, and the other nine seems a perfectly natural event when one considers the significant role "Our Road" has played over many centuries.

However, the revered designation was achieved only after many years of committed effort on the part of many. Historians, lawmakers, and private citizens have worked diligently toward this goal for decades. Commissions and committees have been formed, and countless meetings held, on behalf of this most historic road. Even Sam Houston, way back in 1839, realized the importance of the well-traveled thoroughfare, and presented a Bill to the Senate and House of Representatives of the Republic of Texas "for the reopening of the great San Antonio Road from Nacogdoches to Bexar..declaring it a Public Highway." The Bill was adopted on December 13, 1839, with directions that "the Road Commissioners of the Counties through which said road passes... are hereby charged to reopen and keep in repair said road." [56]

Efforts to save the road in 1913, 1916, 1929, 1939 and later decades provided the necessary foundation for today's legislators, agencies, organizations and interested citizens to finally achieve success. In 1998, a major focus on attaining National Trail status for *El Camino Real* began, immediately gaining public support throughout Texas and the nation.

Prominent in the successful passage of Senate Bill 2052 was its sponsor, Senator Kay Bailey Hutchison of Texas. Similar legislation in the U.S. House of Representatives (H.R. 4122) was introduced by Congressmen Rodrigues,

Sandler, Turner, Ortiz, Frost, Green and Doggett. The bills became Public Law 108-342.

When passage was certain, Senator Hutchison said, "Preserving this landmark enhances our heritage and culture, which is why I first proposed this important measure designating *El Camino Real de Los Tejas* as a National Historic Trail...the law authorizes the National Parks System, working under the Department of the Interior, to designate, establish and maintain the trail."

She stated further that state agencies such as the Texas Historical Commission would be allowed to take part in establishing and designating the trail in order to promote tourism and economic development. Sen. Hutchison then commented, "This legendary trail forged the way for the early development of Texas into a Spanish colony, an independent Republic, and finally, our nation's 28th state. This corridor is not just a highway, it is the foundation of an inspirational past and, with this designation, will become an even more important academic and economic aspect of Texas."[57]

Those patriotic Texans who have gone before, working diligently so that *El Camino Real de los Tejas* might never be forgotten, would be proud of her achievement as a National Historic Trail.

Let's always remember them...when we are *Reminiscing the Road*.

NOTES

1. Lila Kerr, "The Caddo Indian Mounds," excerpts from presentation to East Texas Historical Association, Nacogdoches, Texas, Fall 2005

2. Mrs. Lipscomb Norvell, *King's Highway, The Great Strategic Military Highway* (Firm Foundation, Mrs. Lipscomb Norvell, 1945) pp. 30-34

3. Donald E. Chipman, *Spanish Texas: 1519-1821* (University of Texas Press, Austin, 1992) p. 113

4. *Nacogdoches Sampler, Nacogdoches Chamber of Commerce, Summer 1992*

5. Chipman, *Spanish Texas,* pp. 120-121

6. John D. Inclan, *Biography of Captain Louis Juchereau de St. Denis* (Internet, from Galveston Genealogy Finds, undated)

7. *Los Adaes State Historic Site*, publication of State of Louisiana, Department of Culture, Recreation and Tourism

8. Norvell, *King's Highway,* pp. 27-28

9. Donald E. Chipman and Harriet Denise Joseph, *Notable Men and Women of Spanish Texas* (University of Texas Press, Austin, 1999) p. 195

10. Chipman and Joseph, *Notable Men and Women*, p. 196

11. Chipman and Joseph, *Notable Men and Women*, p. 201

12. W.T. Block, "A Buccaneer Family in Spanish East Texas," *Texas Gulf Historical and Biographical Record*, 1993, Volume XXVII, pp.77-95

13. Edna McDaniel White, *East Texas Riverboat Era* (LaBelle Printing & Engraving Co., Beaumont, 1965) p. 62

14. Louis E. Nardini, *No Man's Land: A History of El Camino Real* (Pelican Publishing Co., New Orleans, 1961) p. 81

15. Nardini, *No Man's Land*, p. 83

16. Nardini, *No Man's Land*, pp. 93-94

17. Nardini, *No Man's Land*, p. 112

18. William Tellis Farmer, *A Centennial History of Sexton Lodge, 1860-1960* (Published by Sexton Lodge, Sabine County, Texas, 1960) p. 17

19. Farmer, *Sexton Lodge,* p. 17

20. Willie Earl Woods Tindall, *Religion: Recollections and Reckonings* (Stephen F. Austin Library, Nacogdoches, Texas, 1976) p. 10

21. Tindall, *Religion,* p. 12

22. Tindall, *Religion,* p. 26

23. Tindall, *Religion,* p. 37

24. Clyde McQueen, *Black Churches in Texas, A Guide to Historic Congregations* (Texas A&M Press, College Station, 2000) p. 115

25. McQueen, *Black Churches in Texas,* p. 119

26. McQueen, *Black Churches in Texas,* p. 120

27. Pearl Travis,"History of Chireno," *Daily Sentinel, Heritage Section,* January 1, 1989

28. Bob Bowman, *Best of East Texas* (Lufkin Printing Co., Lufkin, Texas, 1980) p. 32

29. Archie P. McDonald, *Texas, All Hail the Mighty State* (Eakin Press, Austin, 1983) p. 59

30. McDonald, *All Hail the Mighty State,* p. 61

31. George L. Crocket, *Two Centuries in East Texas,* (Southwest Press, Dallas, 1932) p. 132

32. McDonald, *Texas, All Hail the Mighty State,* p. 61

33. Crocket, *Two Centuries in East Texas,* p. 145

34. Crocket, *Two Centuries in East Texas,* pp.144-146

35. Robert Cecil McDaniel, *Sabine County, Texas: The First One Hundred and Fifty Years* (Texian Press, Waco, 1987) p. 30

36. Margaret S. Henson and Deolece Parmelee, *The Cartwrights of San Augustine* (Texas State Historical Association, Austin, Texas, 1993) p. 87 and p. 208

37. Herman Ehrenberg, *With Milam and Fannin in Texas: The Adventures of a German Boy in Texas' Revolution* (Pemberton Press, Austin, Texas, 1968) pp.14-15

38. Martha Gill Roberts Pay, quotes from Elisha Roberts Family History Collection

39. William Seale, *San Augustine in the Texas Republic* (reprint, Texas State Historical Association, from January 1969 issue, *Southwestern Historical Quarterly*) p. 7

40. Ralph Smith, *The Life of Alexander Horton*, Master of Arts Thesis, University of Texas, Austin, Texas, August, 1936, pp. 16-17

41. Travis, "History of Chireno," *Daily Sentinel, Heritage Section*, January 1, 1989

42. Alton Holt and Willie Thorp et al, *Memories of Chireno* (Chireno Historical Society, 1994) p. 19

43. Linda Cheves Nicklas, *Abstracts of Early East Texas Newspapers, 1839-1856* (Southern Historical Press, 1994) p. 6

44. Texas State Highway Department, *A Guide to Points of General and Historic Interest in Division Number 11* (Texas State Highway Department, Lufkin, Texas, 1936) p. 15

45. Texas State Highway Department, *A Guide to Points of General and Historic Interest in Division Number 11*, p. 20

46. Nicklas, *Abstracts of Early East Texas Newspapers*, selections from *The Red Lander*, *Nacogdoches Times*, and The *Nacogdoches Chronicle*, 4-51

47. *Nacogdoches Daily Sentinel, Heritage Series, Celebrating the 75th Anniversary of Stephen F. Austin State University*, August, 1998

48. The Alto Herald, *Two Hundred and Fifty Years: A History of Alto, Texas 1686-1936* (The Alto Herald, 1936) p. 10

49. The Alto Herald, *A History of Alto*, p. 10

50. Nicklas, *Abstracts of Early East Texas Newspapers*, p. 46

51. Norvell, *King's Highway*, Introduction

52. Norvell, *King's Highway*, p. 16

53. Norvell, *King's Highway*, Dedicatory page

54. Martha Frasher, "Portrait of Mrs. Norvell Will Hang in State Senate Chamber" (*Beaumont Enterprise*, February 21, 1950)

55. Norvell, *King's Highway*, Reports to Mrs. Norvell from Surveyor V.N. Zivley, letters dated December 6, 1915 to October 23, 1916, pp. 216-227

56. Norvell, *King's Highway*, p. 14

57. Senator Kay Bailey Hutchison, *Capital Comment*, October 1, 2004

BIBLIOGRAPHY

Alto Herald, *Two Hundred Fifty Years: A History of Alto, Texas, 1686-1936*, The Alto Herald, 1936

Awbrey, Betty Dooley and Dooley, Claude, *Why Stop? A Guide to Texas Historical Roadside Markers*, Taylor Trade Publishing, Fifth Edition, 2005

Bowman, Bob, *The Best of East Texas*, Lufkin Printing Company, Lufkin, Texas, 1980

Carter, Hodding, *Doomed Road of Empire: The Spanish Trail of Conquest*, McGraw-Hill Book Company, New York, London, Toronto, 1963

Carter, Kathryn Turner, *Stagecoach Inns of Texas*, Eakin Press, Austin, Texas, 1994

Chipman, Donald E., *Spanish Texas: 1519-1821*, University of Texas Press, Austin, Texas, 1992

Chipman, Donald E. and Joseph, Harriet Denise, *Notable Men and Women of Spanish Texas*, University of Texas Press, Austin, Texas, 1999

Clay, John V., *Spain, Mexico and the Lower Trinity*, Gateway Press, Baltimore, Maryland 1987

Crocket, George L., *Two Centuries in East Texas*, Southwest Press, Dallas, Texas 1932

Ehrenberg, Herman, *With Milam and Fannin: The Adventures of a German Boy in Texas' Revolution*, The Pemberton Press, Austin, Texas 1968

Ericson, Carolyn Reeves and Devereaux, Linda Ericson, *Antonio Gil Y'Barbo, Father of Nacogdoches*, private printing, 1995

Ericson, Joe Ellis, *East Texas: A History from Indian Settlements to Statehood*, Heritage Books, Bowie, Maryland, 2002

Farmer, William Tellis, *A Centennial History of Sexton Lodge No. 251*, Sabine County, Texas, 1960

Henson, Margaret S. And Parmelee, Deolece, *The Cartwrights of San Augustine*, Texas State Historical Association, Austin, Texas, 1993

Hickey, Eddie Price, *Elijah Price Family History*, Cornelia Price story related by Mrs. Margaret Porcher Wade to Mrs. Beet Price, 1949, unpublished documents

Holt, Alton and Thorp, Willie, *Memories of Chireno*, Chireno Historical Society, 1994

Jackson, Jack, *Indian Agent, Peter Ellis Bean in Mexican Texas*, Texas A&M University Press, College Station, Texas 2005

Lytch, William E., *The Cradle of Texas Presbyterianism*, Providence House Publishers, Franklin, Tennessee, 1993

McDaniel, Robert Cecil, *Sabine County, Texas: The First One Hundred and Fifty Years, 1836-1986*, Texian Press, Waco, Texas, 1987

McDonald, Archie P., *Texas: All Hail the Mighty State*, Eakin Press, Austin, Texas, 1983

McGraw, A. Joachim, Clark, John W. Jr., Robbins, Elizabeth A., *A Texas Legacy: The Old San Antonio Road and Camino Reales, A Tricentennial History*, Texas State Department of Highways and Public Transportation, Austin, Texas, 1991

McQueen, Clyde, *Black Churches in Texas: A Guide to Historic Congregations*, Texas A&M University Press, College Station, Texas 2000

Metz, Leon C., *Roadside History of Texas*, Mountain Press Publishing Company, Missoula, Montana, 1994

Nardini, Louis E., *No Man's Land: A History of El Camino Real*, Pelican Publishing Company, New Orleans, Louisiana, 1961

Newcomb, W.W., *The Indians of Texas From Prehistoric to Modern Times*, University of Texas Press, Austin, Texas 1993

Nicklas, Linda Cheves, *Abstracts of Early East Texas Newspapers, 1839-1856*, Southern Historical Press, Greenville, South Carolina, 1994

Norvell, Mrs. Lipscomb, *King's Highway: The Great Strategic Military Highway*, Private Printing, Mrs. Lipscomb Norvell, 1945

Pay, Martha Gill Roberts, *Papers and Related Stories of Elisha Roberts Family,* from private family documents, 2006

Seale, William, *San Augustine in the Texas Republic*, Texas State Historical Association, originally published in the January 1969 issue, Southwestern Historical Quarterly

Shealy, Joy, collected research papers and maps, compiled 1990-2005, unpublished

Smith, Ralph, *The Life of Alexander Horton,* Master of Arts Thesis, University of Texas, Austin, Texas, August, 1936

Texas State Highway Department, *A Guide of General and Historic Interest in DivisionNumber 11*, Lufkin, Texas 1936

Tindall, Willie Earl, *Religion: Recollections and Reckonings*, Stephen F. Austin State University, Nacogdoches, Texas, 1976

Truett, Joe C., *Land of Bears and Honey: A Natural History of East Texas*, University of Texas Press, Austin, Texas, 1984

White, Edna McDaniel, *East Texas Riverboat Era*, LaBelle Printing and Engraving Company, Beaumont, Texas, 1965

PERIODICALS

Chinquapin, A Folklore-History magazine, Douglass Independent School District, 1976-77

Texas Co-op Power Magazine, Association of Texas Electric Cooperatives, April, 1996

INTERNET SOURCES

Handbook of Texas Online, General Libraries at the University of Texas and Texas State Historical Association

Block, W.T., "A Buccaneer Family in Spanish East Texas," *Texas Gulf Historical and Biographical Record*, 1993, Volume XXVII

Inclan, John D., *Biography of Captain Louis Juchereau de St. Denis, 1674-1744*, Genealogy Finds, Galveston, Texas, undated

PART II

Lobanillo Swales on Texas State Highway 21 East

INTRODUCTION

I can think of no better authors to write in this series than John and Betty Oglesbee. Both native residents of San Augustine, they returned to their hometown after their educations were completed and served and, in Betty's case, continue to serve as community leaders, activists, and "the keepers of the historical narrative." I first met John Oglesbee when I came to Stephen F. Austin State University and began to work with the East Texas Historical Association. Tall, handsome, and the possessor of one of the most booming and melodious voices I have ever heard, John was a larger-than-life figure. When I became the Executive Director of the Association in 2008, I knew John was one person I had to have in my corner. But I needn't have worried, as John Oglesbee supported whatever and whoever had the best interests of ETHA and East Texas in mind. I looked forward to seeing John when he came to our annual meetings or when we met together in San Augustine to discuss his many civic endeavors toward preserving that city's rich history. I was saddened by John's passing in 2016. We lost a huge voice—both figuratively and literally.

It would probably be difficult to be a partner to such a person as John, but his wife Betty is more than up to the task. Possessed with the same determination to preserve, serve, and chronicle her civic heritage, Betty Oglesbee continues today to be an outsized influence on all who come in contact with her. When Betty decides to get something done, be it raising money, or a commitment toward a reconstruction of *Mission Nuestra Señora de los Dolores de los Ais,* or supporting the preservation of San Augustine history, she approaches it with gusto. I almost wrote "like a bulldog," but that would not do justice to the graceful, dignified, woman I know and have come to cherish.

So, when Betty Oglesbee approached me about a year ago expressing a desire to update her and John's seminal *Reminiscing the Road (El Camino Real de los Tejas from Los Adaes to the Trinity River)*, perhaps the best of many in our Ann and Lee Lawrence Series on East Texas History, I told her, "just tell me what you want me to do." The resulting edition is one that adds to the rich tapestry of the earlier narrative on the *El Camino Real de los Tejas,* a road that even over three hundred years later still runs through some of the most historic stretches in Texas. I know that you will enjoy the new update and look forward to that day when Betty calls me to say that she is ready to revise her and John's work for a third time!

M. Scott Sosebee, Executive Director
East Texas Historical Association

PART II

The Ensuing Years...2008 to 2023

Time goes by so quickly. Sixteen years have passed since *Reminiscing the Road, Volume 7* in the Ann & Lee Lawrence Series for the East Texas Historical Association, was published. Then-ETHA Executive Director Dr. Archie McDonald suggested that the focus of this volume should be the Eastern Texas section of *El Camino Real de los Tejas National Historic Trail*, from *Los Adaes* in Robeline, Louisiana to the Trinity River in Texas.

The result for John and me was both rewarding and fun, as we embarked upon the adventuresome journey of coming to know a host of interesting people who told compelling, memorable stories of events both historic and timely relating to the ancient trail.

Then, during the October 2022 meeting of ETHA in Nacogdoches, Executive Director Dr. Scott Sosebee and I discussed a second edition of *Reminiscing the Road*, bringing up-to-date the remarkable happenings along the *Camino Real* since 2007. In recent years there appears to be quite a renewed interest in the Spanish Colonial period of Texas History.

Appropriately, several noted historians and educators with first-hand knowledge, expertise and professional experience in their given fields of endeavor were invited to contribute to the update of *Reminiscing the Road*. They are:

- Weldon McDaniel, Chairman, Sabine County Historical Commission
- Jeff Williams, GIS Aided Archaeological Research of *El Camino Real de los Tejas* with Focus on the Landscape and River Crossings along *El Camino Carretera*, 2007 Master's Thesis
- Steven Gonzales, Executive Director, *El Camino Real de los Tejas National Historic Trail Association*
- Amanda McVay, Site Manager, *Mission Dolores State Historic Site*
- Rachel Galan, Assistant Site Manager, *Caddo Mounds State Historic Site*
- Dr. George Avery, President, Friends of *Mission Dolores,* Director, Archaeology Lab, Stephen F. Austin State University

Sincere Thanks to All!
Betty Oglesbee

Recent drawing of *El Camino Real de los Tejax National Historic Trail*
Sketch by Kim Whitton

Chapter Thirteen

Reflections and a Look at the Future

by

Weldon McDaniel, 2023

Since its establishment in 1691, the *El Camino Real*, Kings Highway, or the Royal Road has often been referred to as The Trail. Being one of the oldest established trails in the Lower Forty-Eight, it has seen hundreds of thousands of travelers from the Native Americans in the early years to a large percentage of all early Texas pioneers that entered the Province of Texas at the old Pendleton Crossing located on the Sabine River that forms the boundary between Sabine Parish, Louisiana and Sabine County, Texas.

For many years numerous efforts to mark The Trail were carried out by several governmental entities both state and federal, but none have endured and lasted like the famous "five mile markers" set by the Daughters of the American Revolution and the State of Texas in 1918. These pink granite markers every five miles mark The Trail starting at the old Pendleton Crossing on the Sabine River all the way to the Rio Grande River that forms the boundary between Texas and the Republic of Mexico. None of these efforts marked the famous northern route through Sabine County that crossed the Sabine River at the old Carter's Ferry location that was located two-and-one-half miles above/ up-river or northeast of the Pendleton Crossing.

This northern route split from the southern route, Pendleton Crossing, at the large spring near old Camp Sabine/Block House Road described in the Stephen F. Austin diary dated 15/16th of July 1821 on his first trip into the Province of Texas. This location is behind the Beulah Baptist Church/Cemetery south of Toledo Town and on the eastern side of the Sabine River bottom. From this location the split-off turns northwestward and crosses the Sabine River at the Merritt's Mountain/Carter Ferry location. This location can be seen looking north at the east end of the Pendleton Bridge.

For many years this ferry was operated by William Stephen Bradford Carter (1832-1899) and wife Elizabeth Margarete Mason Carter (1855-1889). Before the Carters, the ferry, established in the late 1700s, had been operated by Patterson, Pugh and Michael Crow. Pictured is the only known photo of the old Carter's Ferry. The low river banks made it easy for wagons and travelers to approach the ferry.

William Stephen Bradford Carter and wife Elizabeth Margarite Mason-Carter

Up-river from the Carter's Ferry, the northern route entered Texas in the vicinity of what is today Best Park and traveled west, State Highway 276/Carter's Ferry Road, to Geneva. Three miles west of Geneva the northern route rejoined the southern route where today the Wagon Swales/Tracks Park and Hiking Trail are located. Just east of this location, the King's Road Cutoff rejoins the southern route.

In 2014 the National Park Service started a program to "sign" the *El Camino* from Natchitoches, Louisiana to the Rio Grande River. Sabine County was one of the first in Texas to sign the original route from Pendleton Crossing to Milam and then to Geneva. These signs are every two miles, one facing west and one facing east.

In 2022-2023 the northern route, State Highway 276/Carter's Ferry Road and the King's Road, received signage from the National Park Service.

Carter's Ferry

Although this planning has been in the works for a while, a new development on The Trail at the old Pendleton Crossing was started in 2022 by the Sabine River Authority of Texas. This project will see a new six-lane boat ramp, a curved brake-water for protection of the boat ramp when boats are present, parking lots, a children's playground, ball courts, restrooms, a walking trail, an administration building, Texas Department of Transportation addition of turning lanes into this development for safety reasons, and other recreational facilities. All of this development is within site of the old Pendleton Crossing/ Gaines Ferry location.

The plans for this project will also include a new port-of-entry building to welcome visitors into Texas. This port-of-entry will offer tourists information, displays outlining the history of the *El Camino Real*, history of the Pendleton Crossing, a history of Sabine County plus displays of historic artifacts recovered at the crossing in 2006 when the Toledo Bend Reservoir water level was down twelve feet. One of the really exciting additions to this project will be the preservation and signage of pioneer wagon tracks/swales that exist on this property. Hopefully more development will come in the future.

In 1812 James Gaines began operating the Pendleton Ferry. During the years 1815-1840 he built two identical houses, the Gaines Ferrying House and the Gaines-Oliphint House. The houses were moved in the late 1960s as the waters of Toledo Bend Reservoir covered the old Pendleton crossing. Of the two, the Gaines-Oliphint house survived, and is now located on a two-acre site near Pendleton Harbor. Fully restored, it is an exemplary example of the earliest Pre-Republic of Texas architecture.

The Gaines-Oliphint House.
Drawing by Kim Whitton

Chapter Fourteen

El Camino Real de los Tejas National Historic Trail Association
and the
Lobanillo Swales

Steven Gonzales has served *El Camino Real de los Tejas National Historic Trail Association* as its Executive Director since 2007, when the organization was begun for the purpose of building a strong citizen support group for the Trail. A few years later, the discovery of the Lobanillo Swales, a four-acre tract of land bordering *El Camino Real* (Highway 21 East) in Sabine County became the springboard for a partnership between the Association and the National Trails Intermountain Region of the National Park Service.

Executive Director Gonzales described the *Lobanillo Swales* as "a collection of seven remnants of the Royal Road in the forest of East Texas. The site was essentially a super-highway, with some swales measuring 18 feet deep and 12 feet wide...the *Lobanillo Swales* represent cultural human pathways imprinted into the landscape via pack mule, cart, wagon, and foot from the 1700s to the early 1900s. The swales are the best known physical remnants of a path that has long existed as one of the most ancient roads in American history."

The project began in 2013, when a crowdfunding campaign raised money to purchase the site at an auction held June 4, 2014 on the steps of the Sabine County Courthouse. Coordination with the National Park Service led to appropriate steps in developing the property, and later, to archaeological investigations during the winter and spring of 2015.

Gonzales continued: "By October of that year, the NPS-NTIR developed a conceptual plan for the site titled, 'Lobanillo Swales—Interpretive Retracement Trail Development Concept Plan.' By mid-2016, landscape architects from the NTIR were drafting construction level documents for amenities such as the parking area and trailhead. By May 2017 the landscape architect team had surveyed and staked the site for development. Lobanillo was on its way to being visitor-ready! In November 2017, Sabine County provided labor and equipment to improve the roadway into the site and develop the parking area and trailhead. The final piece of the puzzle came together in April 2018. Activities included the development of a quarter-mile loop hiking trail, installation of interpretive panels, and installation of site identification and roadway directional signage to the site."

The *Lobanillo Swales Park* was dedicated on April 16, 2018 with an impressive attendance, celebratory speeches by Aaron Mahr from the National Trails Intermountain Region of the National Park Service, and Brad Patterson from the Texas Historical Commission, who remarked, "We know in Texas that many are heritage travelers, who go out and seek places like *Lobanillo Swales*." Sabine County Judge Daryl Melton commented, "We are a hidden jewel, and a sounding board for actually promoting tourism in our county." Steven Gonzales said, "Lobanillo is an exciting place, and it is the most dramatic place anywhere along the road that we've found where there are physical remnants of a road right here on the landscape." KTRE-TV's Donna McCollum reported that "Lobanillo is now a Texas Antiquities Landmark. The National Park Service has placed it on the National Register of Historic Places."

Long before the *Lobanillo Swales* became famous as the newest reminder of Spanish Colonial history in this locale, Historian Extraordinaire Weldon McDaniel had introduced John and me to the "swales." Located ten miles east of San Augustine and just over the Sabine County line, we visited the site often, John always with camera in hand, photographing the impressive swales in every season of the year.

Weldon and his friend Felix Holmes, with the assistance of Sabine County workers, cleared the acreage, built the parking lot, installed culverts where needed, and improved the entrance road to the property, all with the blessing of Sabine County Judge Daryl Melton. The Trail Association employed noted archaeologist Dr. Sergio Iruegas to investigate the site. A crushed granite walking trail overlooking a section of swales was carefully constructed and approved by the National Park Service in order to take full advantage of the site's historical elements. Exhaustively researched interpretive signage, with maps, timelines, and early history, accurately tell the entire story. A third sign was added early in 2020 with additional clarifying information.

The *Lobanillo Swales*, 10 miles from San Augustine, Texas, on Highway 21 East

Raiford Stripling's sketch of *Mission Dolores*, considered the most authentic of all architectual images.

Chapter Fifteen

Mission Dolores State Historic Site
Mission Nuestra Senora de los Dolores de los Ais

Mission Dolores has been a prominent, visible locale within the city limits of San Augustine for more than three centuries. The site of the *1721 Mission Nuestra Senora de los Dolores de los Ais* was a part of Edmund Quirk's land bordering the Ayish Bayou and intersecting *El Camino Real de los Tejas*... an area chosen first by the Ais Indians, then by Spanish missionaries as early as 1717, and finally by American immigrants who arrived via the ancient trail during the early 1800s. In 1832 when settlers approached Edmund Quirk offering to purchase 640 acres of his four-league Spanish land grant for the town site of San Augustine, he voiced some objection, as he had promised to give the old mission property to his grandchildren. After much consideration, Quirk finally accepted their offer of $200 for this land, according to Dr. George L. Crocket, author of *Two Centuries in East Texas*. Today, *Mission Dolores State Historic Site* is a familiar landmark, only four blocks from downtown San Augustine and the Courthouse Square, surveyed according to the American Plan by Thomas McFarland in 1833.

Mission Dolores was one of six missions situated along *El Camino Real de los Tejas National Historic Trail* to solidify Spain's claim to the desirable lands adjoining the road, and as a deterrent to likely French intrusion. Father Antonio Margil de Jesus, president of the Zacatecan friars, was the driving force in organizing three of the East Texas missions: *Mission Guadalupe* in Nacogdoches, *Mission San Miguel* near Robeline, Louisiana, and *Mission Dolores* in San Augustine. His reputation was already well established with the founding of at least twenty-five missions in Mexico and Central America prior to his joining the 1716 expedition into eastern Texas led by Captain Domingo Ramon. Father Margil was a man of magnificent, compelling stature, with feet reportedly "as tough as mule's hooves" from walking barefoot. Traveling along, he enthusiastically sang the *Alabado*, praise of God and the saints.

Fr. Antonio Margil de Jesus.
Sketch by Kim Whitton

His inspiring renditions of the traditional Catholic chants became the best-loved songs of the Indians.[1]

Always the most humble of priests, Father Margil signed his letters:
"La misma nada" (Nothingness itself)

The East Texas missions built in 1716 and 1717 were closed in 1719, when the news of war between Spain and France created the fear of French encroachment into Spanish Texas. Dr. Crocket reported the critical condition as follows: "Father Margil hastily buried his iron tools and implements, gathered up his church ornaments, and headed for *Mission Concepción*, having dispatched his lay brother to warn the other missions."[2]

"When the Marquis de San Miguel de Aguayo was appointed Governor of Texas and *Coahuila* he was also commissioned to lead the expedition to reoccupy and reestablish the deserted missions of East Texas. He began to assemble his forces in October 1720…The Marquis de Aguayo succeeded in marshaling the most formidable array that entered Texas during the eighteenth century. He enlisted five or six hundred men whom he divided into eight companies with a captain for each…He had nearly four thousand horses and six hundred mules loaded with clothing, arms, ammunition, etc., including six cannon…Three standards bearing the pictures of several saints were blessed by the ecclesiastics, one of the standards inscribed with the motto, 'Fight for the Faith and King'."[3]

According to Aguayo's diarist de la Pena, Father Margil had been waiting for an opportunity to join such an expedition. As they continued on from *Mission Guadalupe* (Nacogdoches), de la Pena noted:

> "Father Margil went ahead with a detachment in order to build the next mission, that of *los Dolores.*
>
> "We continued the march toward the east-northeast, through a broken and wooded country, until we had advanced one-fourth of a league beyond the spot on which had stood the *Mission of Nuestra Senora de los Dolores de los Ais,* of which not a vestige remains. To Father Margil this new site for the mission seemed preferable, because it is on the banks of a stream that has its source nearby, and because it is on an elevation, without trees, and near a large tract of level land that can be used for cultivation.

"The next day was spent in building the church, all the men necessary being employed.

"The occasion was celebrated with the same solemnity as at the previous missions, and after the High Mass and the salute from all the companies, Fray Antonio Margil and the captain of the Indians were presented title of possession. The captain was clothed as other Indian captains had been, and the Indian men and women were clothed also as at the other missions. His Lordship (Aguayo) added joy to the occasion by offering the Padres and captains a splendid meal. One hundred and eighty Indians were clothed at this mission, and Father Jose Albadadejo remained here.

"The Governor having left a detachment here to finish the church and to build the dwelling for the Padres, we set out toward the east." [4]

In 1727, Father Pedro Munoz, a Catholic priest, described the Church at *Mission Dolores* as beautifully furnished and decorated with the appropriate colors required by the Catholic Church. The Church and other buildings in the mission compound (probably a total of seven) were well-constructed, neat, clean, and functional. Writings of historian Carlos E. Casteneda show that there were "70 families of some 300 Indians, most of which did not live at the mission," but in their own dome-shaped, thatched huts nearby. In all, there were eight tribes within five miles of *Mission Dolores*. Although characterized as lazy and shameless in many respects, the Ais cooperated with the padres in tending the crops, and the women helped with household chores. [5]

Sad to say, the indefatigable efforts of Father Margil and those who followed him met with limited success among the Ais Indians. Over the years, the Ais were glad to accept food and medical assistance, but not religion. Records confirm that over a 36-year period there were only 158 baptisms, many of which were of a deathbed nature. Unfortunately, the natives associated death with the baptismal water. [6]

Mission Dolores closed in 1773, thus ending its Spanish Colonial history. Many considered this mission, and others, a failure. From a different vantage point, the Marques de Rubi noted that the "Ais Indians spoke Spanish almost without exception, that they were very wise, that they learned to use modern implements, raise good crops independently, and were skilled in the use of firearms."[7] In addition, *Mission Dolores* had served over the years as a convenient way station between *Los Adaes* and Nacogdoches.

As noted earlier, *Mission Dolores* has been a familiar presence in San Augustine for centuries. Over the past fifty years, San Augustine County Historical Society, San Augustine County Historical Commission, the City of San Augustine, local citizens and historians have worked in concert to accomplish their dream of a full-scale reconstruction of the *Mission Dolores* compound. Archaeological investigations have been conducted by Dr. Kathleen Gilmore, University of North Texas in 1972-73, and James Corbin, Stephen F. Austin State University, Nacogdoches in 1976, 1977, and 1978. When San Augustine historian Julia Wade learned that SFA's new archaeologist would be coming soon, she asked that a note be attached to the door of his office with an urgent plea for help, and her phone number. Jim Corbin received Julia's message before having time to unpack his boxes.

In 1993, A Master Plan for *Mission Nuestra Senora de los Dolores de los Ais* was prepared for the City of San Augustine by Architect Joe C. Freeman and Archaeologist Nancy Kenmotsu, Texas Historical Commission. Recommendations were in four phases: Phase I, Archival, Archaeological, Site Development, Visitor Center; Phase II, Archive and Laboratory, Site Development; Phase III, RV Park; Phase IV, Mission Reconstruction and Construction of Caddoan Hamlet. Phases I, II, and III are complete. Phase IV is on the horizon!

An Advisory Committee of local citizens and City Manager Alton Shaw were appointed for planning and developing the *Mission Dolores* site. In 1994, the Texas Transportation Commission selected the City of San Augustine's proposal for the development of a Visitor's Center, RV Park, and Museum at the site of *Mission Dolores*. The $2.5 million project was subsequently funded through the Texas Statewide Transportation Enhancement Program, a part of the Intermodal Surface Transportation Efficiency Act (ISTEA), and the City of San Augustine. The museum inside the Visitor's Center was made possible through a grant from the T.L.L. Temple Foundation, and a video presentation prepared by Bob Bowman Associates provided an in-depth visible interpretation of the Spanish Colonial period in Texas History. Amid much publicity and excitement, opening ceremonies for the *Mission Dolores* Visitor Center and Museum were held on January 9, 1999.

The Texas Beyond History website provides a wealth of information relating to *El Camino Real de los Tejas*, as well as *Mission Dolores*. In February

2012, Jeff Williams, Forestry Department, Stephen F. Austin State University, was cited by this excellent online source as follows:

> "In the piney woods of East Texas, James Corbin and Jeff Williams rank as the primary researchers of the *Camino Real*. Corbin published in the groundbreaking volume edited by Al McGraw, John Clark, and Elizabeth Robbins entitled, *A Texas Legacy: The Old San Antonio Road and the Caminos Reales, A Tricentennial History, 1691-1991*. Williams 2007 Master's Thesis (GIS Aided Archaeological Research of *El Camino Real de Los Tejas*) stands as the most comprehensive work on the subject to date…in the fall of 2007, Texas Historical Commission archaeologist James Bruseth recommended that additional investigations be conducted to more precisely determine the size of the mission complex. In spring 2008, Williams identified a swale at *Mission Dolores*, which makes *Mission Dolores* the third public area in Texas which has a remnant of *El Camino Real de los Tejas* that visitors can experience firsthand—the other sites being *Mission Tejas State Park* and *Caddo Mounds State Historic Site*…The swale or rut discovered at *Mission Dolores* in 2008 is a lingering physical trace of an old road that was created by many travelers over a long period of time. Worn into the ground, the swale is a shallow-to-deep U shaped linear depression created by heavy carts or wagons pulled by draft animals like oxen or mules…In the spring of 2008, Dr. George Avery, with Jeff Williams and Connie Hodges, conducted a shovel testing survey covering both the Gilmore and Corbin excavation areas… Jim Bruseth and his team conducted geophysical surveys in the area, including magnetometer, metal detector, and ground-penetrating radar surveys…Three and a half decades after she last worked at *Mission Dolores*, Dr. Kathleen Gilmore visited the Avery investigations in the spring of 2008…and brought her rare insight and unique perspective to discussion of the survey results…Corbin's old road feature and a newly identified swale all indicated that originally, *El Camino Real* passed right through the middle of the mission compound. Much like Highway 147 does today." [8]

Jeff Williams penned these meaningful words in describing the passage of *El Camino Real* through the City of San Augustine and *Mission Dolores*: "The old road had solid rock fords for crossing the Ayish Bayou, there were clear running springs that were cool and sweet, there were tall grasslands and dense woodlots, and by the time of the Spanish and French, there was a well-known east to west pathway linking kinship bands of the Caddo."

The City of San Augustine owned and operated the entire *Mission Dolores* complex during the years 1994 to 2016. On January 28, 2016, Mission *Nuestra Senora de los Dolores de los Ais* was acquired by the State of Texas as its 21st Historic Site, and was a seamless transition from ownership by the City of San Augustine to the State of Texas. The ribbon cutting ceremony and dedication were held at *Mission Dolores* on September 9, 2016, with Texas Historical Commission Chairman John L. Nau II, THC Executive Director Mark Wolfe, State Senator Robert Nichols, and State Representative Trent Ashby, Mayor Leroy Hughes, and City and County officials present for the event.

Mission Dolores Site Manager Amanda was interviewed by Justin Mott of KTRE-TV for a documentary program in April 2023. Amanda McVay said, "Since *Mission Dolores* has been designated a State Historic Site, the museum, gift shop, and all educational venues have been totally and beautifully renovated. The completely new museum features interactive elements, new orientation video, and an expanded gift shop. On the grounds of the historic site, new interpretative signage and improved walking trails have been updated. Visitors can enjoy time on the grounds through the campground or the two picnic pavilions, both complete with fireplaces for cold-weather events, and a disc golf course for relaxed entertainment. There are 32 overnight campsites that feature full hook-up, back-in spaces. Listed in the National Register of Historic Places, *Mission Dolores* site has been designated a State Antiquities Landmark. It is located on the *El Camino Real de los Tejas National Historic Trail.* Many years of archaeological research have proven that the ancient roadway passes right through the middle of the original 1721 *Mission Dolores* compound."

The Friends of *Mission Dolores State Historic Site* Association's purpose is to be an organization of interested persons to advance and encourage participation, understanding, enjoyment, and public use of the educational and cultural programs and facilities of *Mission Dolores State Historic Site.*

The Association works in conjunction with *Mission Dolores Site Staff* to receive and maintain funds to promote the history of the site, including acquainting the community with the needs of *Mission Dolores State Historic Site*, and to support the initiatives and programs being provided. FOMD is very active, meeting often and always cognizant of needs and assistance that can be provided by this Association. Memberships in this organization are welcome!

After more than fifty years of striving toward a full-scale, authentically-as-possible reconstruction of *Mission Dolores*, this long-awaited dream is now on the brink of realization. Thanks to the efforts of Senator Robert Nichols and State Representative Trent Ashby, the 2023 Texas Legislature budgeted $800,000 for the *Mission Dolores* reconstruction project.

It is interesting to note that Texas Restoration Architect Raiford Stripling's conceptual drawing of *Mission Dolores* is considered by the Texas Historical Commission the most accurate depiction of the fenced compound, with chapel, priests' quarters, soldiers' quarters, and other assorted structures. Stripling was special friends with Miss Henrietta Henry, President of the Texas Old Missions and Forts Association, who had traveled to Spain and reported to him her discoveries. Raiford's son Ray (Raggy) Stripling had given his father's architectural drawings to Texas A&M University, his Alma Mater. Representative Trent Ashby contacted Dr. Gregory Luhan, Dean of Architecture, Texas A&M, who is now on board with his students to assist with the *Mission Dolores* reconstruction project.

Texas Historical Commission's J. Brett Cruse and *Mission Dolores* Site Manager Amanda McVay have compiled a comprehensive document entitled "Historical and Archaeological Overviews of *Mission Dolores de los Ais* and Costs Estimates to Recreate a Representation of the Historic Mission." Spanish Colonial construction methods, prevalent in Texas during the 1700s mission period, will be featured throughout, using all native materials. Additional staff will be provided for educational tours, maintenance, and special events. Thus, *Mission Dolores* will become a destination for travelers of every age and inclination who will enjoy the new museum, tour the "reconstructed" mission, and take advantage of the extensive educational opportunities that this historic site will provide.

Notes for Chapter Fifteen

1 Hodding Carter, *Doomed Road of Empire,* McGraw Hill Publishers, 1963. p. 71.

2 George L. Crocket, *Two Centuries in East Texas*, Southwest Press, Dallas, Texas, 1932, p. 24.

3 Crocket, pp. 26-27.

4 James E. Corbin, Arlan Kalina, and Thomas C. Alex, Appendix by Kathleen Gilmore, *MISSION DOLORES DE LOS AIS, Archaeological Investigations of an early Spanish Colonial Mission,* San Augustine County, Texas. Stephen F. Austin State University and Texas Antiquities Committee, September 1980, pp 226-227.

5 Adan Benavides, Jr., *Archival Investigations for Mission Nuestra Senora de los Dolores de los Ais, San Augustine County, Texas,* Austin, Texas 1998, p. 235.

6 Corbin, p. 237.

7 Corbin, p. 237.

8 Quotes from www.texasbeyondhistory.net/dolores/camino.html.

Burial Mound at Caddo Mound State Historic Site
located near Alto, Texas
Image provided by Rachel Galan

Chapter Sixteen

Caddo Mounds State Historic Site
An El Camino Real de los Tejas destination
before there was a Camino Real

by
Rachel Galan

Across rivers, wetlands, woods, and prairies, the Caddo (*Hasinai, Natchioches, and Kadohadacho confederacies*) hunted, traded, traveled, and lived along the road the Spanish coined *El Camino Real de los Tejas*, the royal road to the *Tejas*—a reference to the Hasinai Caddo of East Texas. For over 1,000 years, It was the beat of Caddo drums, voices raised in songs, stories, ceremonies, and all the other sounds of life and death that infused the earth of the east Texas Road crossing modern day Caddo Mounds State Historic Site (CMSHS). During the mid- 19th century, the Caddo living in east Texas were forcefully pushed out of the area by Anglo settlers and displaced Native groups. Many Caddo headed west where they lived for about 10 years on a reservation in the Brazos River Valley. In 1859, on a Caddo trail of tears, these people from a civilization once hundreds of thousands strong survived that journey. Today, the Caddo Nation of Oklahoma, situated in Binger, Oklahoma, has more than 7,000 enrolled members.

In the beginning, led by Moon, the first Caddo man and the first Caddo woman emerged from the Earth carrying a drum, fire, pumpkins, and corn. They led many Caddo to settle and thrive on lands in modern day Texas, Louisiana, Arkansas, and Oklahoma. The stories and cultural landscape from more than 1,000 years of Caddo triumph and tragedy, intersected by European exploration and colonization, and Anglo settlement, are now told by the Texas Historical Commission (THC). In 2008, the THC acquired 397 acres of ancestral Caddo homeland from Texas Parks and Wildlife and the Texas Forest Service. Over the last fifteen years, CMSHS staff have nurtured relationships and partnerships with Caddo people informing the development of structures, educational programs, site interpretation, cultural preservation and land conservation initiatives.

In October of 2014, the THC opened a remodeled museum at CMSHS with new hands-on experiences for visitors, exhibits that highlighted Caddo history and modern Caddo, and expanded walking trails. An original segment of *El Camino Real de los Tejas*, still visible at CMSHS, received official National Trail markers and new interpretive signs. During the summer of 2016, site staff and community volunteers joined Caddo elder Phil Cross and his apprentice Chad Earles to build a traditional Caddo grass thatched house. The grass house was furnished with Caddo-made and other items for interpretive purposes. The goal of the design was to provide an authentic experience for visitors while having a functional space for educational programs. In 2017, during the Caddo Culture Day event, for the first time in 800 years, Caddo artist Chase Kawinhut Earles prepared a Caddo dish in a traditionally made clay cooking pot, over a fire, in a traditional Caddo grass house. Videographer Curtis Craven (Hecho A Mano Productions) documented the complete house construction process from raw material selection and collection to final thatching. Funded by the THC, Curtis crafted the footage into a 30-minute documentary airing on PBS. In December 2019, "Koo-Hoot Kiwat: The Caddo Grass House" won the prestigious Lone Star Emmy for Texas Heritage.

The Caddo response to the grass house project was overwhelming. Participation in CMSHS's annual Caddo Culture Day event grew substantially and there was a significant increase in Caddo interest in partnering with other site projects including the development of Snake Woman's Garden, an interpretive garden of traditional food, fiber, and medicinal plants. Individual Caddo contributed heirloom seeds, planting traditions, and traditional recipes.

Shaho' is the Caddo word for the tornado experience. On April 13th, 2019, CMSHS was devastated by an EF3 tornado that hit during the annual Caddo Culture Day celebration. Among the approximately 85 people at CMSHS when the tornado hit were Caddo elders, children, artists, members of the tribal government, and the keepers of the traditional songs, dances, language, and the knowledge and skills to do beadwork and make regalia. The tornado injured many, some critically, and destroyed the museum and Caddo grass house. Although modern buildings crumbled, the ancient Mounds and Snake Woman's Garden (*Keekah Natee Toots'ah Naht'ooh*) remained. As Snake Woman's Garden grew into a tangle of food and medicine, alive with the work of pollinators, and home to nesting birds, it became an important symbol of resilience and renewal.

Enrolled Caddo Nation member and elder, Kay O'Neal, tells her *shaho'* story as a retelling of the Caddo creation story. As she stood looking back at the fallen museum, she witnessed her people emerging from the rubble, dressed in their regalia, carrying the things precious to them, reliving the original Caddo creation story. The much altered landscape offered a new canvas for the THC, a strong community of Caddo and East Texas survivors, and their supporters to rebuild structures and programs together. At a July 2019 CMSHS Teacher's Workshop and Community Healing event, the 25 Caddo in attendance joined other community members to express their commitment to rebuilding the grass house. They voiced their deep ties to CMSHS, their ancestral homeland, and the importance of their involvement in rebuilding the site. Grass house construction was set to begin in 2020/2021, but plans were delayed due to the COVID pandemic and the suspension of in-person activities. In the summer and fall of 2022, a team of five Caddo women, under the leadership of Kay O'Neal and guidance from Phil Cross, worked with community volunteers and site staff to build a new Caddo grass house at CMSHS. Alongside the building of the grass house, contractors were hard at work on the new Caddo Mounds museum and visitor center. The new museum at CMSHS offers hardened areas for storm safety, design elements informed by Caddo input, and many exhibit materials created by Caddo artists. Snake Woman's Garden is home to the *shaho'* memorial, offering a beautiful space for survivors and visitors to reflect and remember.

2023 will welcome the start of a new *El Camino Real de los Tejas*-focused project funded by the National Park Service to tell the history of this ancient road through a Caddo lens. In addition to new interpretation, NPS funding will allow for increased accessibility for visitors of all ability levels to the *Camino Real* trails.

The Friends of Caddo Mounds volunteer organization has supported CMSHS in all of its initiatives. Anyone interested in getting involved with ongoing and future CMSHS projects can contact the site for more information, 936.858.3218.

The Grass House at Caddo Mounds State Historic Site
Image provided by Rachel Galan

EPILOGUE

And thus, my legacy continues…

I am *El Camino Real de los Tejas National Historic Trail.* The passage of time has not diminished my importance as the vital artery of influence and transport for more than three centuries!

My very existence is an enduring, vibrant reminder of times past and of days yet to come, as my ancient trail ribbons over hills and streams, through forests, fields of grain, verdant pasturelands, and the arid climes of our Texas landscape.

And so, I invite you to join me on my centuries-old chosen pathway. Let us experience together the ambience of times long gone, and the excitement of new discoveries ahead, as we visit the welcoming sites along the way!

May we take time to breathe in the still-lingering aura of those countless souls who traveled this historic trace before us, and remember them…as we are…

Reminiscing the Road

www.ingramcontent.com/pod-product-compliance
Lightning Source LLC
Chambersburg PA
CBHW061800070526
44586CB00023B/2647